Lorraine –
Thank you very much for lending me your nice wok. (Sorry for the mis-spelling!)

Imelda

Macramé Plus

By Imelda Manalo Pesch

Techniques • Wrapping
Coiling • Rug-Hooking
Weaving • Crocheting
Knitting • Stuffing

Materials • Ceramics • Metal
Enamel • Shells • Glass
Wood • Feathers • Beads
Bells • Fur • Jars • Bottles
Driftwood • Bamboo

STERLING PUBLISHING CO., INC. NEW YORK
Oak Tree Press Co., Ltd. London & Sydney

OTHER BOOKS OF INTEREST

Appliqué and Reverse Appliqué	Family Book of Crafts
Art Nouveau Embroidery	Finger Weaving: Indian Braiding
Bargello Stitchery	Giant Book of Crafts
Beads Plus Macramé	Hooked and Knotted Rugs
Big-Knot Macramé	Inkle Loom Weaving
Corn-Husk Crafts	Macramé
Create Your Own Natural Dyes	Needlepoint Simplified
Creating from Remnants: Stitchery with Imperfect Fabrics	Net-Making & Knotting
	Off-Loom Weaving
Creative Lace-Making with Thread & Yarn	Patchwork and Other Quilting
	Practical Encyclopedia of Crafts
Cross Stitchery	Spin, Dye and Weave Your Own Wool

All pieces in this book are works of the author unless otherwise indicated.
Photographs by Jon Hand and the author.
Drawings by John Pesch.

Metric Conversion Chart

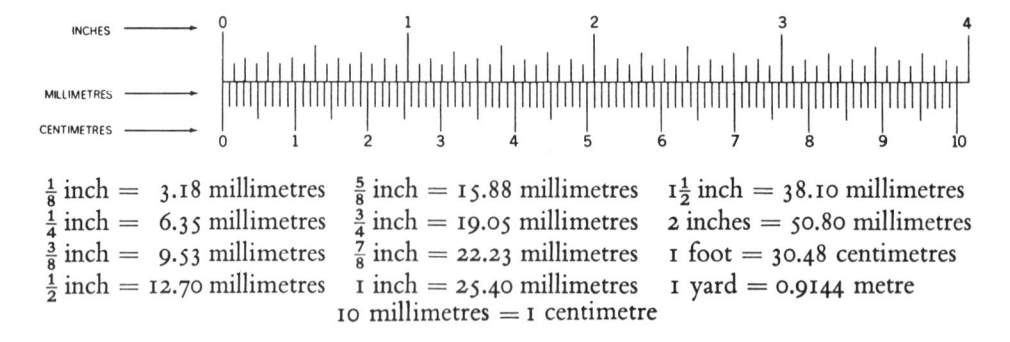

$\frac{1}{8}$ inch = 3.18 millimetres $\frac{5}{8}$ inch = 15.88 millimetres $1\frac{1}{2}$ inch = 38.10 millimetres
$\frac{1}{4}$ inch = 6.35 millimetres $\frac{3}{4}$ inch = 19.05 millimetres   2 inches = 50.80 millimetres
$\frac{3}{8}$ inch = 9.53 millimetres $\frac{7}{8}$ inch = 22.23 millimetres   1 foot = 30.48 centimetres
$\frac{1}{2}$ inch = 12.70 millimetres   1 inch = 25.40 millimetres   1 yard = 0.9144 metre
10 millimetres = 1 centimetre

Copyright © 1976 by Sterling Publishing Co., Inc.
419 Park Avenue South, New York, N.Y. 10016
Distributed in Australia and New Zealand by Oak Tree Press Co., Ltd.,
P.O. Box J34, Brickfield Hill, Sydney 2000, N.S.W.
Distributed in the United Kingdom and elsewhere in the British Commonwealth
by Ward Lock Ltd., 116 Baker Street, London W 1
Manufactured in the United States of America
All rights reserved
Library of Congress Catalog Card No.: 76–1186
Sterling ISBN 0-8069-5350-0 Trade   Oak Tree 7061-2163-5
5351–9 Library

Contents

PART I: MACRAMÉ 5

Introduction 6
   Planning

The Fibres 9

The Basic Knots 12
   Equipment . . . Knotting . . . Square Knot (SK) . . . Flat Knot (FK) . . . Double Knot (DK) . . . Bead Knot or Overhand Knot . . . Collecting Knot . . . Lark's Head Knot . . . Buttonhole Knot

Design and Color 24

Finishing 25

PART II: MACRAMÉ PLUS 27

Macramé Plus Wrapping and Coiling 28
   Wrapping . . . Weed Pot . . . Coiling

Macramé Plus Rug-Hooking 38
   Wall Hanging

Macramé Plus Weaving 44
   Types of Weaving . . . Cardboard Weaving . . . Frame-Loom Weaving . . . Tubular Weaving . . . Wall Hanging

Color Section . . . . opposite page 48

Macramé Plus Crocheting 53
    Increase and Decrease . . . Macramé and Crochet Sculpture

Macramé Plus Knitting 60
    Hand-Knitted Hanging

Macramé Plus Stuffing 67
    Stuffed Wall Hanging

Macramé Plus Anything 70
    Macramé, Bead and Silver Neck Piece

Conclusion 75

Suppliers 76
    United States . . . Canada . . . Denmark . . . England . . . Finland . . . New Zealand . . . Norway . . . Sweden

Cover Pictures Guide and Captions 78

Index 80

Part I: Macramé

Introduction

Of the many methods of converting fibre into fabrics that have been developed through the centuries, macramé (hand knotting) in particular has become extremely popular among contemporary textile craftspeople. It is one of the most versatile and potentially exciting crafts.

Macramé has been used, to a large extent, for decorative rather than functional purposes. You can use it alone as a pure technique, or you can successfully combine it with various other textile crafts and materials, so that the knotting becomes an important part of your work. If you do not limit yourself to macramé alone, but also explore the related crafts (such as knitting, crocheting or weaving), working them together, you can create not only imaginative macramé projects, but beautiful "fabric-art" pieces as well. Experiment with several different textile techniques and combine them to enrich the surface interest of your work and explore new materials, both natural and synthetic. If you do not confine yourself to traditional, representational forms, it is easier to concentrate on the esthetic values of your art piece rather than on the techniques you employ.

The most popular uses for these "combination creations" are as wall hangings

Illus. 1. This close-up of color Illus. E2 shows macramé combined with weaving. On the left, seeds were worked into the macramé and mohair was woven into the floating macramé cords. In the figure on the right, the cotton cords used in the macramé were also used as warp threads in weaving. The macramé was resumed after the weaving was done.

Illus. 2. One way to plan a fibre creation is to do a rough original sketch, like the one for a wall hanging shown here.

and sculptures. Wall hangings are those fibre constructions which you can hang on or in front of a supporting wall. They are usually thick or deep, like a relief structure, and have a good deal of visual surface detail. Some hangings are two-sided and can be viewed from the back as well as from the front.

Sculptures are three-dimensional and are meant to be either free-hanging or free-standing. You can hang them directly from the ceiling, letting them move freely so that you can observe them from all sides, or you can place them on a base such as a table or pedestal or on the floor. At times, you might want to add supporting materials, such as metal, wood or plastic frames. You may want to stuff your creations with such materials as polyester fibre, kapok, nylon stockings or what-have-you. When the structures are to be self-supporting, you need to work the knots tightly or use firm or tightly spun yarns.

You can create unique pieces of fabric art using fibres and macramé combined with other textile techniques—many different types are illustrated in this book, including such things as weed pots, neck pieces, baskets, collars, dolls and pillows.

PLANNING

You have a choice of ways to plan a fibre creation. You can work entirely from your imagination, letting the threads follow your hands until you have completed the piece. Or, you can begin to plan your project by sketching a rough design first (one of these plans is shown in Illus. 2), and then deciding what techniques will best carry out your intended creation.

Once you have conceived a complete idea, then choose the materials best suited for your project. If at some point, you feel that the methods or material you selected are not working out, put the work aside temporarily, until you find a solution to the problem. Come back to it later with a new approach. This makes much more sense than trying to force a technique to work. Very often, the results of your second attempt will be quite different from your original sketch, and usually much better.

In planning a combined fibre project, think in terms of a symphony. Music and art are closely related: the only difference is that fibre art is concerned with the senses of sight and touch, while music is concerned with hearing. In a symphony, various instruments play together harmoniously, creating a pleasing sound. In a combined fibre piece, various materials and techniques work together harmoniously, creating an exciting piece. Its design is as important as the melody or style in a musical piece. The intensity of its color is as important as the softness or loudness of the sound in music. You express a mood in the warmth or coolness of color, as you do in the tempo of the music. Both forms of art have a textural (smooth or rough) quality.

Dissonance, once considered unpleasant to the eardrums by the classical composers, is used very often in modern music. Contemporary craftspeople, likewise, combine contrasting textures and colors which academic painters once considered in poor taste. Keep this in mind as you plan your color schemes and do not be afraid to try different and unusual combinations.

The pieces shown in this book are intended to stimulate beginning or advanced craftspeople of all ages to explore the various possibilities of combining macramé with one or more different textile crafts. What technique you use is not as important as the results you obtain. Your own innovations actually control the work: the techniques are simply methods you use to obtain a finished creation. You do not have to master all the stitches or knots, as long as you can do the basics of each technique you choose. If you are able to do more elaborate stitches, so much the better—you can easily integrate them into your work. Remember that you are not restricted to the techniques discussed in this book. You can successfully combine any others you know with macramé.

The Fibres

No matter what other techniques you want to combine with macramé, first you need to learn how to tie the simple, basic macramé knots into a variety of arrangements. The knots themselves are different in texture and particularly appealing because of their contrasting characters. People will often explore the knotted surface and actually touch the piece in order to fully appreciate it. Therefore, your choice of fibre materials in the construction of the knotted structure is immensely important.

Examine the yarns and cords which are available, touch them and try knotting them. In this way, you will develop a keen sensitivity to their characteristics, a quality that is essential for you as a crafter. Their texture, as well as their colors and strengths, are very important to consider before you begin work. Have on hand a wide range of yarns, cords or fibres—in an array of colors—to choose from. Note that color is more intense when the fibre is glossy and toned down when it is dull. You can dye natural fibres to achieve special desired colors by using natural or chemical dyes. Some craftspeople also prefer to spin their own yarns.

You can find a multitude of cords or twines—such as cotton, nylon, jute, plastic, linen or sisal—in hardware and marine or upholstery supply shops. You can use rug yarns made of cotton, wool, rayon, polyester and other blends, as well as novelty and hand-spun yarns. They are all readily available from suppliers who specialize in craft materials for weavers, rug-hookers, knotters and needleworkers.

Each project will demand a certain type of material, depending on the character and the intended purpose of the finished article. Generally, ideal macramé cords are firmly twisted with a good body and are strong enough to survive the tension you apply while working the knots. But do not hesitate to experiment with unusual fibres that are unevenly spun with a thick-and-thin or nubby quality. These fibres often add unusual texture and interest to your work.

The qualities of the fibres you use will never limit your creativity, and they can give you ideas for innovations. If you use a variety of fibres, they will add depth and richness to your composition. For example, you can use unusual fibres as Working Threads which you make into Vertical Double Knots or Diagonal Double Knot Bars (which will be discussed later) over the stronger and smoother threads. Take a look at Illus. A1 and the close-up in Illus. 3. Here different weights and

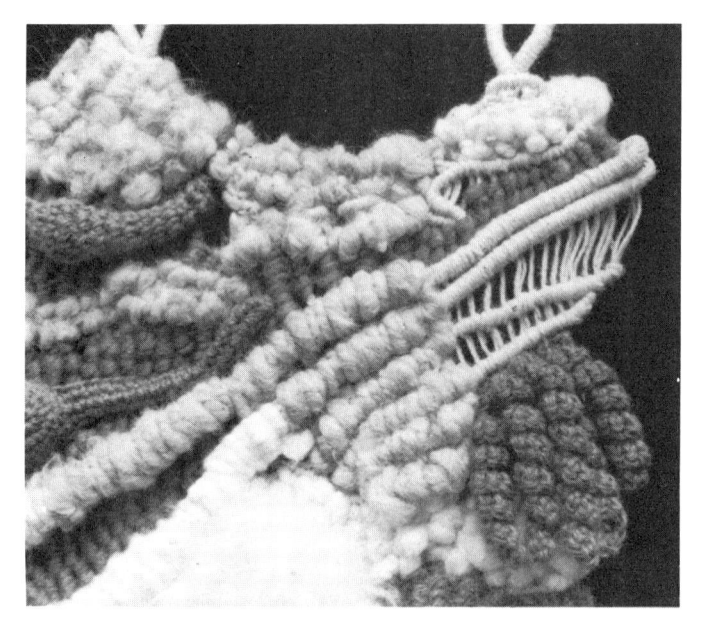

Illus. 3. In this close-up of color Illus. A1, notice the effect created by different weights and textures of Working Threads being knotted over stronger threads as Knot Bearers.

textures of Working Threads were knotted over stronger threads or Knot Bearers for a strikingly textured piece. In Illus. A2, waxed linen was combined with rough linen cord and polished India twine.

When you are selecting yarns for macramé, try to avoid elastic and very soft yarns such as those commercially produced for knitting; they do not hold their form

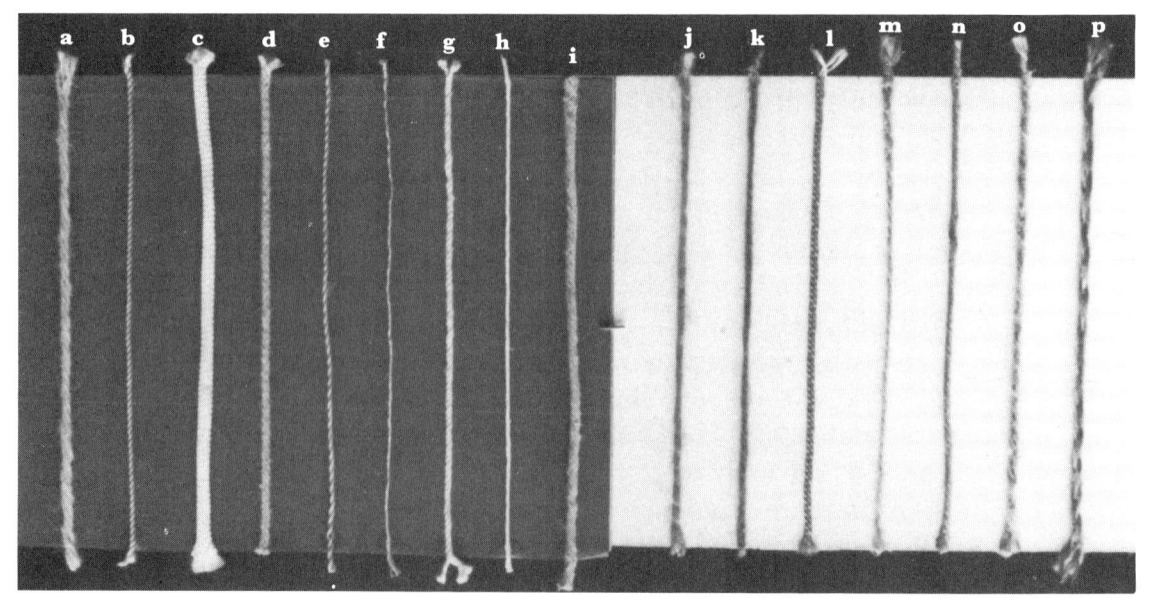

Illus. 4. Some fibres you can use for macramé: *a*: **avanti rug yarn**; *b*: **nylon twine**; *c*: **braided nylon cord**; *d*: **braided cotton cord**; *e*: **medium-weight sisal**; *f*: **light-weight sisal**; *g*: **cotton seine twine**; *h*: **marine cotton cord**; *i*: **upholstery cord**; *j*: **polyester rug yarn**; *k*: **dacron rug yarn**; *l*: **braided rayon cord**; *m*: **jute cord**; *n*: **polished India twine**; *o*: **natural wool rug yarn**; *p*: **rayon wool rug yarn**.

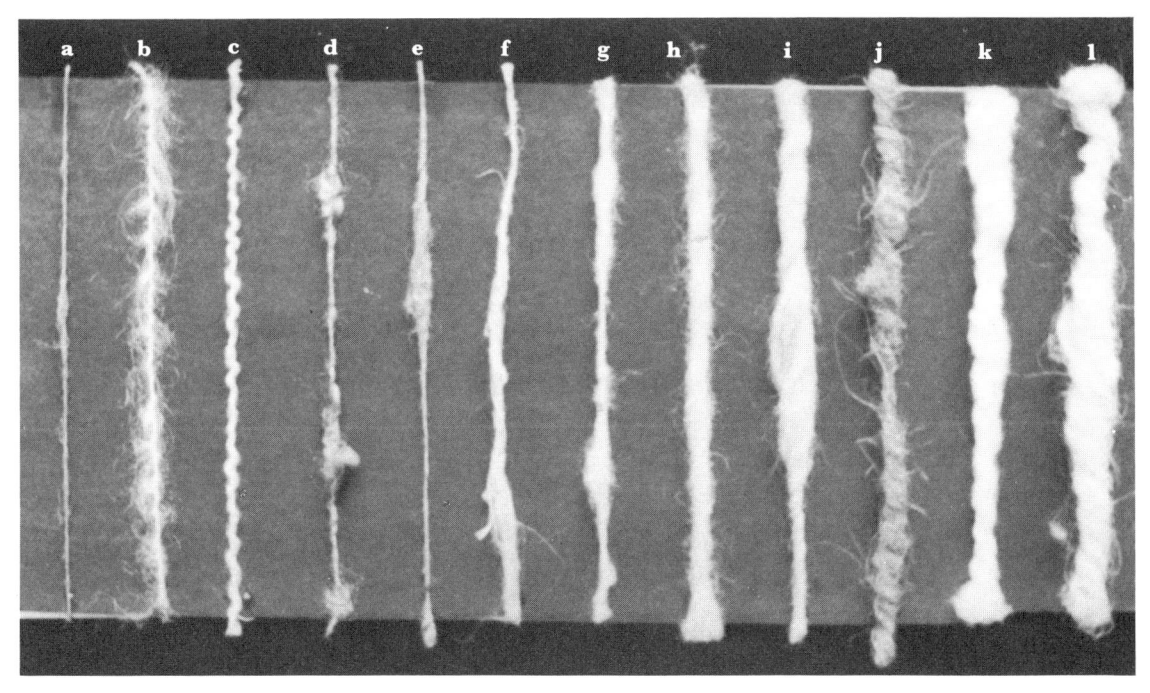

Illus. 5. Additional fibres you can use for macramé: *a:* rough linen; *b:* mohair; *c:* **looped cotton**; *d:* **nubby cotton-rayon**; *e:* **nubby rayon, silk, cotton and jute**; *f:* **nubby rayon**; *g:* **hand-spun nubby wool**; *h:* **home-spun wool**; *i:* **primitive spun wool**; *j:* **camel and goat hair**; *k:* **hand-spun cotton**; *l:* **heavy hand-spun wool.**

when knotted. You also need to be an experienced knotter to work with slippery cords. When you want to work with heavy cord, you may want to consider using two or more strands of the same yarn together. If the piece you are planning will be subjected to some degree of stress, be sure to choose firm or well-twisted yarns, twines, cords or braided cords. Illus. 4 and 5 show various fibres which you can use.

See page 76 for a list of some of the suppliers of fibre materials for macramé, weaving and other creative textile crafts.

The Basic Knots

You can create macramé, like other textile crafts, in different shapes, either flat or cylindrical. Because you work macramé entirely with your own hands, without using any special instruments, you control the tightness of the knots and, therefore, the design itself. As you work the cords, you will discover ways of manipulating them to suit your purposes. If the project you plan will not be subject to stress and tension, such as those you plan to hang or just place on a supporting surface, you can knot it less tightly.

EQUIPMENT

Use a table top or your lap as a working area. You may also want to use a working base on which you can anchor your work to keep it secure during the knotting process. A firm pillow filled with polyurethane foam is ideal for this, because it holds the glass-head pins or T-pins which you use to fasten down the cords. Use a piece of wall board as your base, if a pillow is not available. For heavy or stiffer cords, a wood board with nails fastened to the top, as shown in Illus. 6, makes a good support.

Illus. 6. You can use a wooden board with nails fastened to the top, as shown here, as a working base for your macramé work.

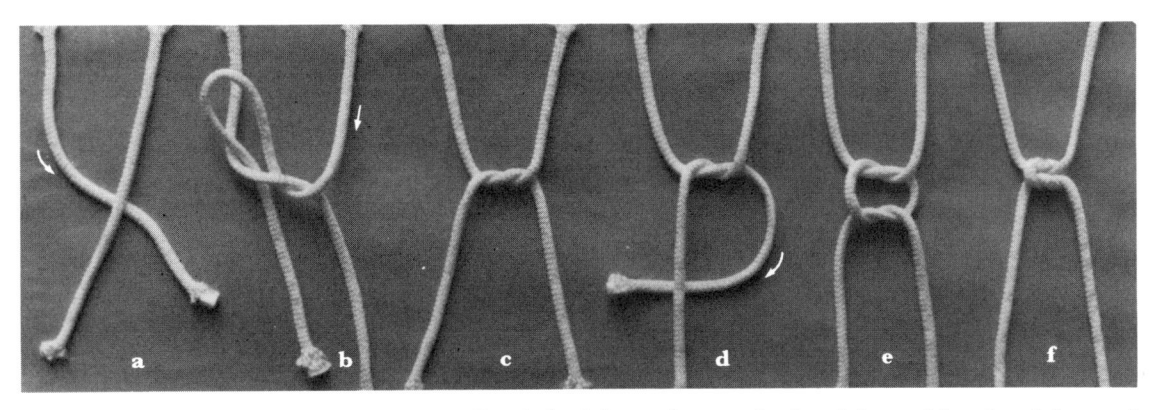

Illus. 7. Formation of a Square Knot. *a:* **Bend the left cord towards the right and lay the right cord over this, straight downwards;** *b-c:* **Then bring the right cord under the left cord, and draw it out to make the first twist or crossing;** *d-e:* **Now do the reverse; bend the right cord towards the left, cross the left cord over and draw it out to make the second crossing;** *f:* **Pull both ends tight with equal tension to complete the Square Knot.**

If you are making a hanging piece, and plan to mount it on a wooden dowel, you can also use the dowel as an anchor for the work while you create it.

You will also need scissors, a crochet hook, a large-eyed needle and a tape measure or ruler.

KNOTTING

The two basic knots which are most versatile in macramé are the Flat Knot (FK), sometimes called the Square Knot, and the Double Knot (DK), sometimes called the Double Half Hitch or Clove Hitch. These names vary according to place and author.

The Flat Knot is quite useful in making net-like designs, as well as narrow strips called "sennits." It is merely a simple Square Knot with two middle cords caught in-between the crossings.

Square Knot (SK)

To make a Square Knot, you interlace two cords. Follow Illus. 7, using practice cords.

a: Bend the left cord towards the right, and lay the right cord over this, straight downwards.

b-c: Then bring the right cord under the left cord, and draw it out to make the first twist or crossing.

d-e: Now do the reverse. Bend the right cord towards the left, cross the left cord over and draw it out to make the second crossing.

f: Pull both ends tight with equal tension. You have completed the SK.

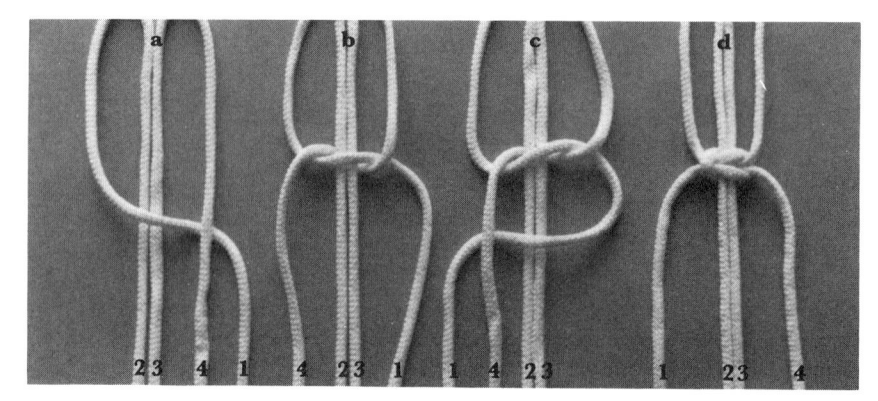

Illus. 8. Formation of a Flat Knot. *a:* Bend cord #1 over cords #2 and #3; place cord #4 over cord #1, straight downwards; *b:* Bring cord #4 under cord #1, then under cords #2 and #3, and draw it out through the left space, between cords #1 and #2; *c:* Pull both ends with equal tension to bring the crossing into position. Now reverse the first step by bending the right cord #1 over cords #2 and #3; place cord #4 over cord #1, straight downwards; *d:* Bring cord #4 under cords #2 and #3; draw cord #4 out through the space between #3 and #1. Pull the ends so that the second crossing lies next to the first.

Flat Knot (FK)

A Flat Knot is made up of four cords: two outer Working Threads (WT) and two filler cords, which are the middle cords. The cords are numbered 1, 2, 3 and 4 from left to right. Follow Illus. 8 and 9 to make this knot.

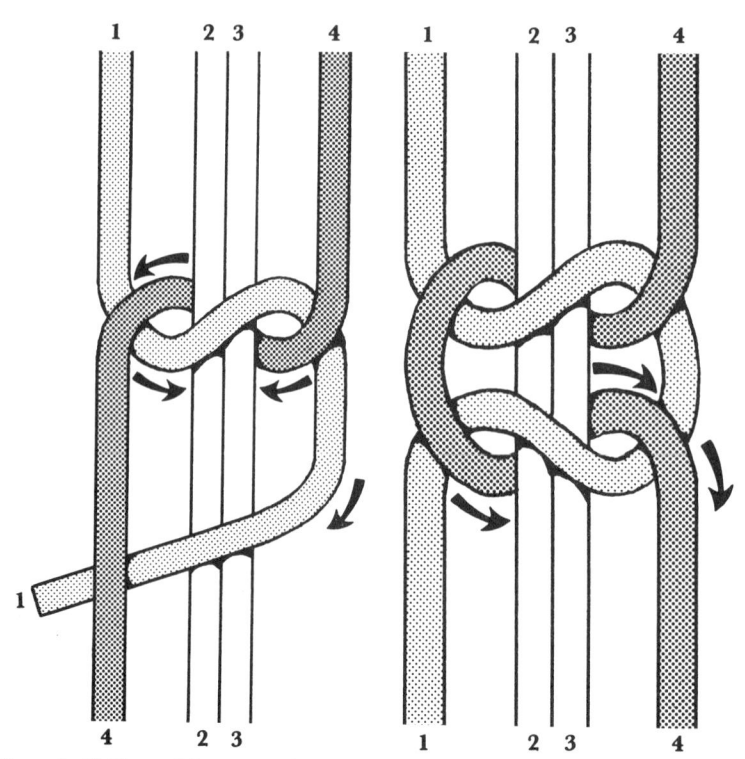

Illus. 9. Follow this to make a Flat Knot, which is composed of four cords, two outer Working Threads and two middle filler cords.

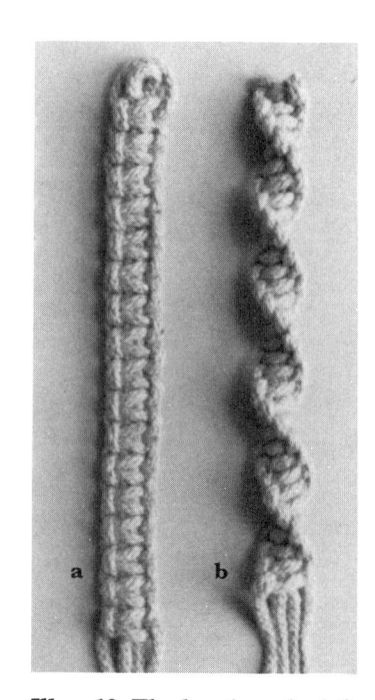

Illus. 10. The band on the left shows a sennit of Flat Knots; the band on the right shows a sennit of Half Flat Knots.

14

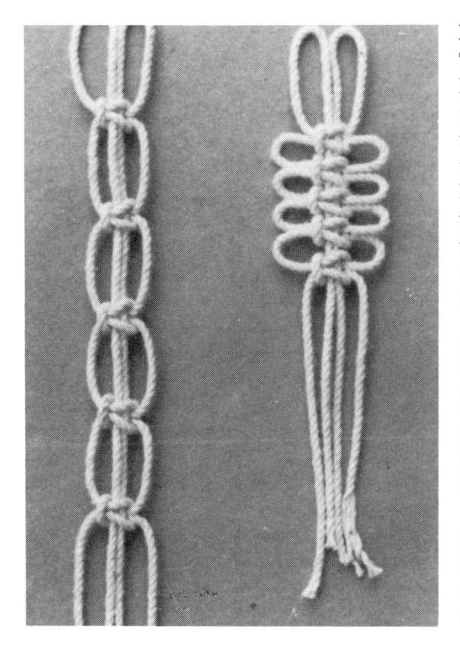

Illus. 11 (left). To make Flat Knots, space them out within the sennit, as was done on the left, or push them up together, as was done on the right.

Illus. 12 (right). The top portion here shows a network of Flat Knots. The bottom section shows different multiples of Flat Knots forming sennits between single knots.

a: Bend cord #1 over cord #2 and #3; place cord #4 over cord #1, straight downwards.

b: Bring cord #4 under cord #1, then under cords #2 and #3, and draw it out through the left space, between cords #1 and #2.

c: Pull both ends with equal tension to bring the crossing into position. Now reverse the first step by bending the right cord #1 over cords #2 and #3; place cord #4 over cord #1, straight downwards.

d: Then bring cord #4 under cords #2 and #3; draw cord #4 out through the space between #3 and #1 (right hole). Pull the ends so that the second crossing lies next to the first crossing. You have completed the FK.

Successive FK's form a band or a sennit of FK's, as shown in Illus. 10a. A sennit of the first half of the FK (Half FK) is also possible, as you can see in Illus. 10b. Notice that this band automatically twists as you make the knots. When making FK or Half FK sennits, only the WT's (outer cords) go into the knot itself, while the middle cords are just filler cords. Therefore, allow longer lengths for the outer cords.

You may use single, double or multiple FK's to make a network or open-mesh design, as you can see in Illus. 12. You can vary the spaces between the FK's or you can set them close to each other. In Illus. H1, for example, the stuffed material was covered with single FK's in a network pattern. In Illus. 11, on the other hand, the Flat Knots were set far apart on the same filler cords within a sennit, and were then pushed up together to form loops along the sides.

You can achieve a three-dimensional effect if you bend FK sennits over to form loops. See Illus. 81 and 120 for good examples of this.

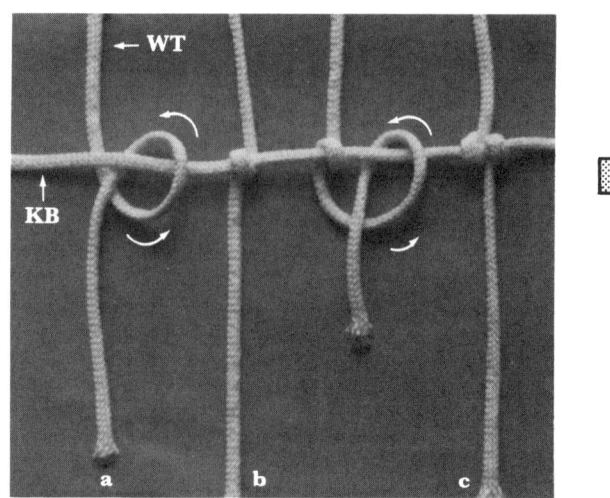

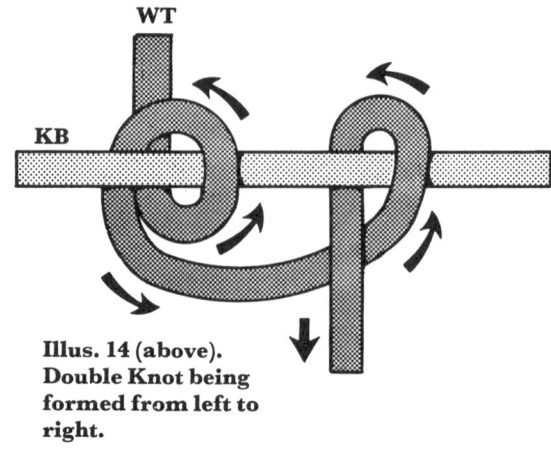

Illus. 13 (left). Formation of a Double Knot. *a:* Pass the Working Thread from under the Knot Bearer over and around towards the left; pull the cord downwards, so the twist lies in place; *b-c:* Repeat to form the second twist.

Illus. 14 (above). Double Knot being formed from left to right.

Double Knot (DK)

The Double Knot, shown in Illus. 13, is very useful in creating different forms and shapes because you can easily drop out cords at any point, behind the knotted work, or add a new cord, whenever you need or want to. You can also create a more solid structure with this knot.

The Double Knot consists of a Knot Bearer (KB) around which you knot the Working Thread (WT). Follow Illus. 14.

a: Pass the WT from under the KB over and around towards the left; pull the cord downwards, so that the twist lies in place.

b-c: Then repeat this. Always hold the KB taut, while you make the two

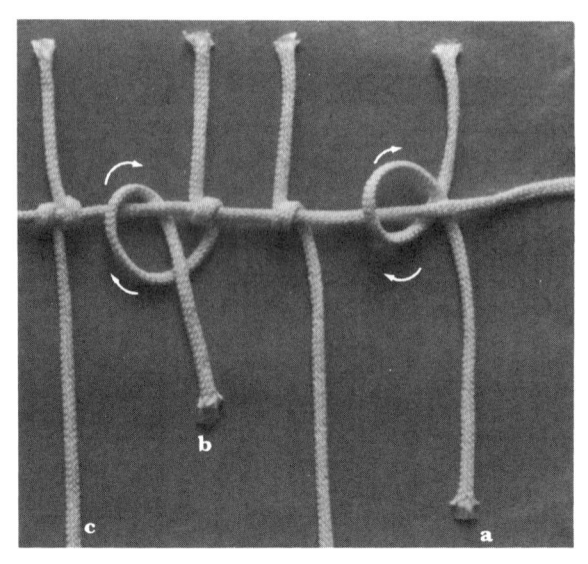

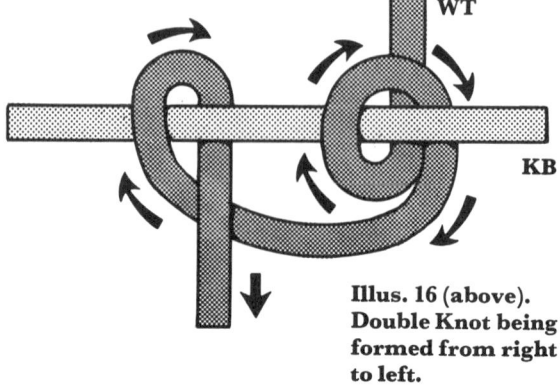

Illus. 16 (above). Double Knot being formed from right to left.

Illus. 15 (left). The reverse of Illus. 13. You can make the Double Knot working towards either the left or the right.

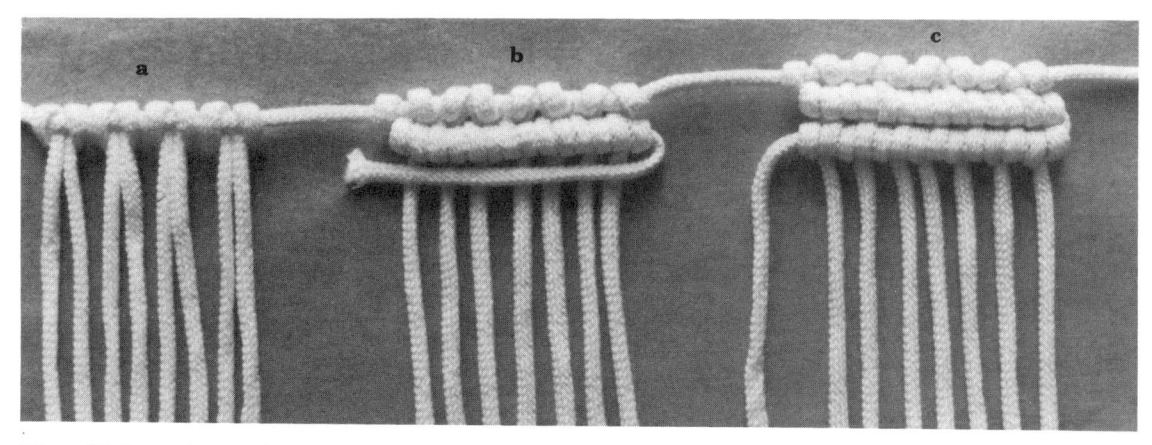

Illus. 17. In *a*, the cords are mounted by using Lark's Head Knots. In *b*, the first cord on the left was used as a Knot Bearer, while each of the other cords were used to form a Horizontal Double Knot Bar. In *c*, the Knot Bearer was brought back to form a second Horizontal Double Knot Bar next to the first one.

twistings. You can make the Double Knot working towards either the left or the right. Follow Illus. 15 and 16 to knot in reverse.

You can make more than one DK with a single KB, to make DK Bars. To make a Horizontal DK Bar, you hold the KB in a horizontal left or right direction. The DK Bar in Illus. 17b was made in a horizontal right direction, while the bar added in Illus. 17c was made in a horizontal left direction. To make a Diagonal DK Bar, hold the KB in a diagonal left or right direction. The DK Bar in Illus. 18a was made in a diagonal right direction; the bar added in Illus. 18b was made in a diagonal left direction. In Illus. 18c and 18d, the DK Bars were continued to make an X.

You can work DK Bars so that they lie close to one another, or you can set them apart with spaces between them. Double or multiple DK Bars may have open or

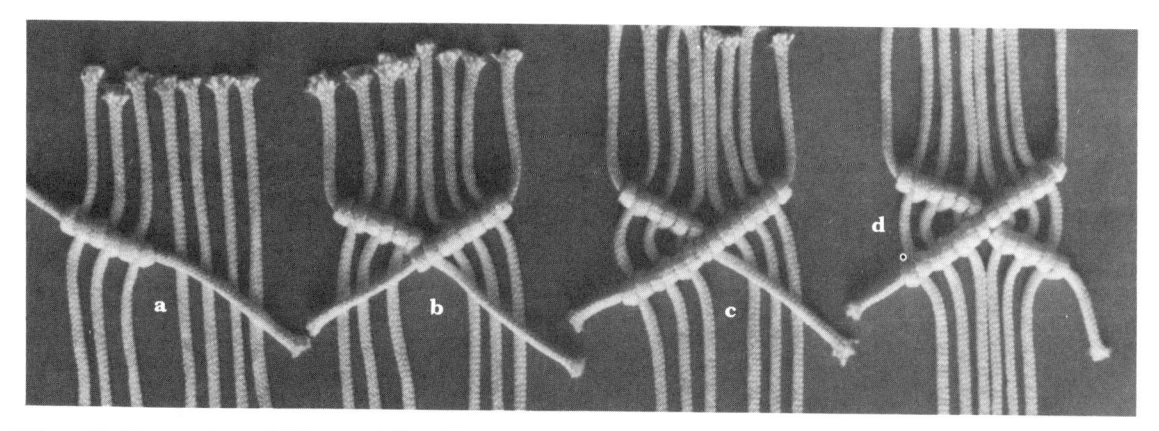

Illus. 18. Formation of Diagonal Double Knot Bars. *a:* The DK Bar was made diagonally towards the right; *b:* The DK Bar was made diagonally towards the left; *c:* The DK Bars were continued in their respective directions; *d:* An X of Diagonal DK Bars was completed.

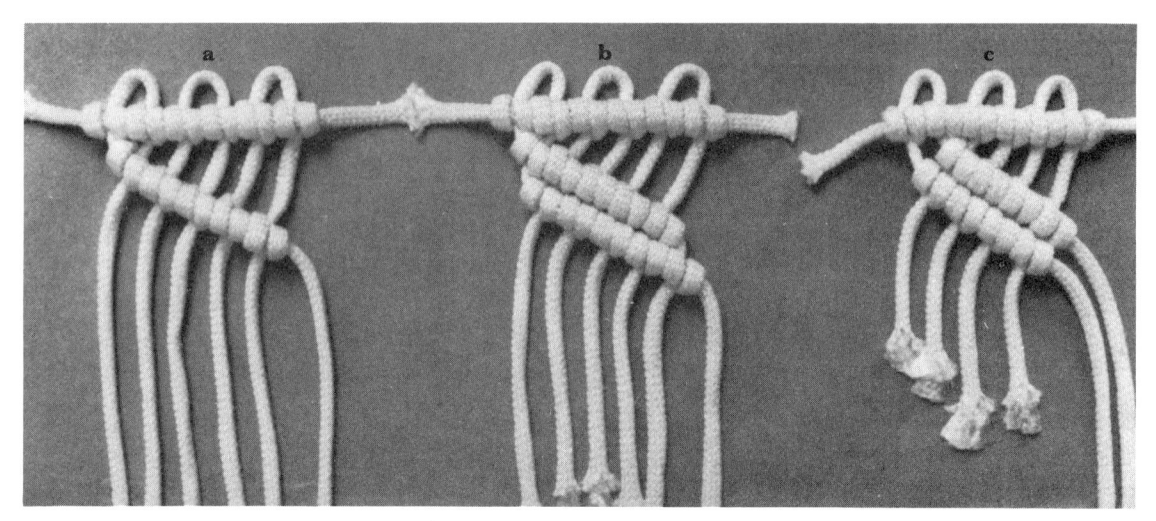

Illus. 19. The Diagonal DK Bars in *b* **are closed, while those in** *c* **are open.**

closed ends. In the DK Bar in Illus. 19b, the ends are closed; in Illus. 19c, the ends are open. You can mix open and closed DK Bars any way you wish.

Another variation is Vertical DK Bars, which you form by holding the KB vertically. Vertical DK Bars are good to use if you want to introduce a new color into your knotted work, as you can see in Illus. 20. Notice that the KB cord is completely covered by the WT in the construction of a DK; therefore, the color of this WT is the color that will be visible on the surface.

See Illus. 21 to 23 for other methods of adding on new cords, using DK Bars.

Illus. 20. Formation of Vertical Double Knot Bars. *a:* **New cords were added to form the Vertical Double Knot Bars;** *b:* **The ends of the first added cord were used to form the second line of Vertical Double Knots.**

Illus. 21. Here, six new cords were added as Knot Bearers. The last Knot Bearers were then pulled together before a Square Knot was made to raise the whole structure.

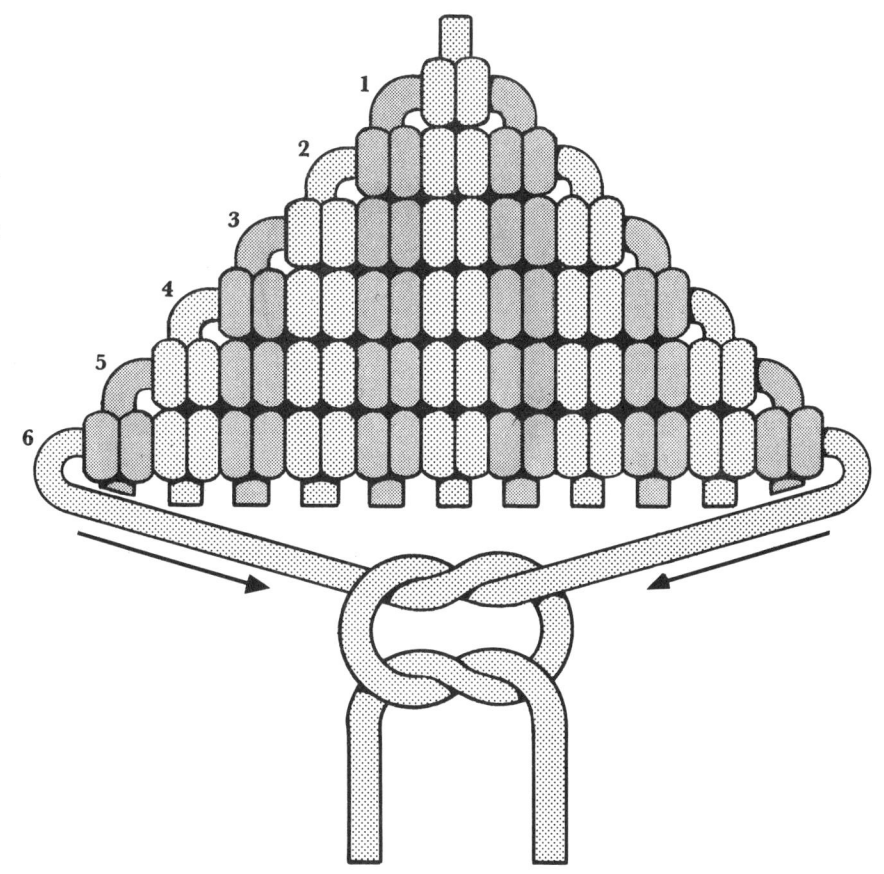

Illus. 22 (below). Five new cords were added. Notice how the Working Threads carry the color on the macramé surface.

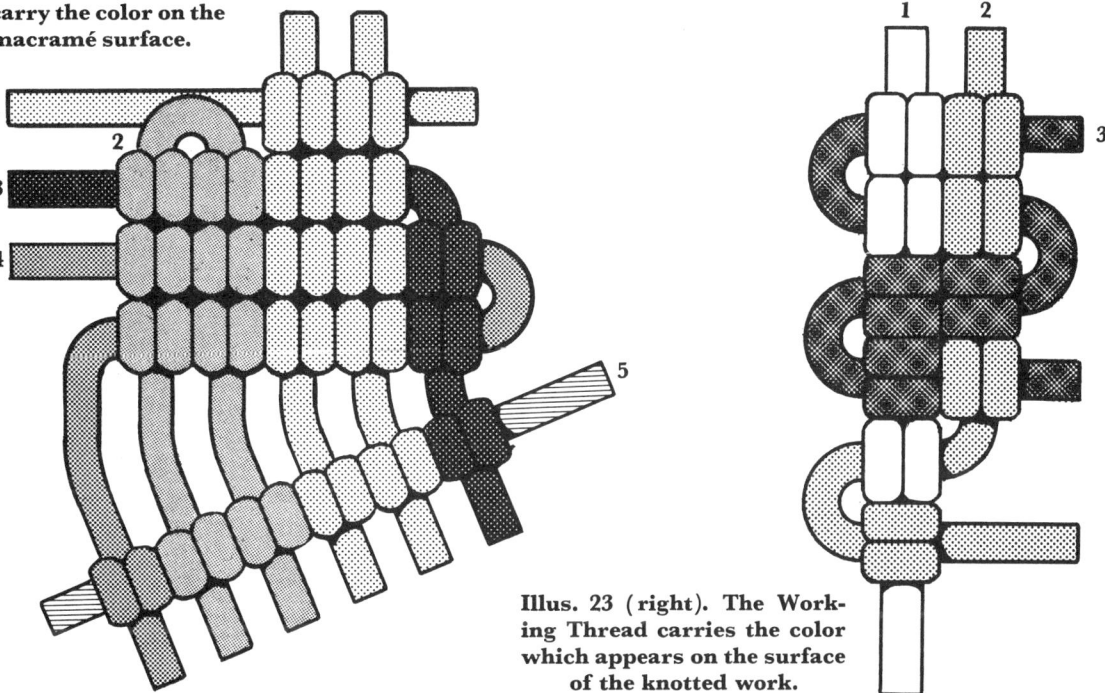

Illus. 23 (right). The Working Thread carries the color which appears on the surface of the knotted work.

19

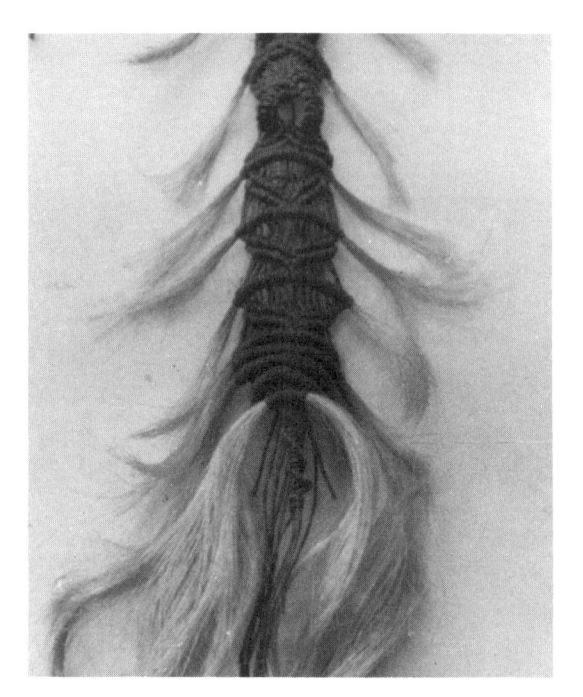

Illus. 24. Loose sisal fibres were used as Knot Bearers to form curved Double Knot Bars.

Illus. 25. This close-up of Illus. 117 features Double Knot Bars made in different directions to form flat and raised areas.

Illus. 24, 25 and 26 show some ways you can utilize Double Knot Bars in the construction of different structures.

Illus. 26. In this close-up of color Illus. E1, Double Knot Bars were mixed with Flat Knots and Single Buttonhole chains. Two weights of polished India twines were used.

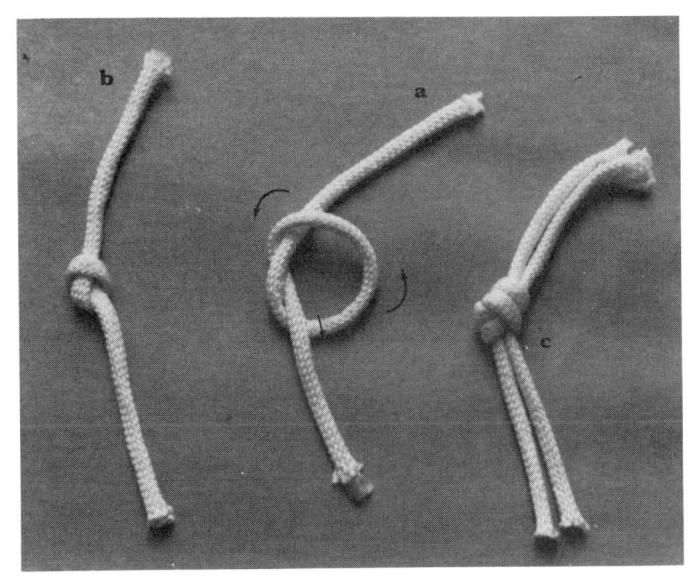

Illus. 27. **Formation of a Bead Knot.** *a:* Bring the cord around itself, and then draw it through the space to form the knot; *b:* A single-strand Bead Knot; *c:* A double-strand Bead Knot.

Bead Knot or Overhand Knot

To make a Bead Knot, bring one or more strands around itself. Then draw the end through the space or hole you have made. Illus. 27 shows how to make a Bead Knot. In the neck piece in Illus. J3, the Bead Knots were used to simulate beads.

Collecting Knot

The Collecting Knot, shown in Illus. 28, is useful in bundling cords together to form a fringe-like finish on a macramé piece.

a: Twist a side cord around the group of cords, and draw it through the space or hole you have made.

b: Then pull it tightly in place.

c: Repeat in order to make a more secured knot.

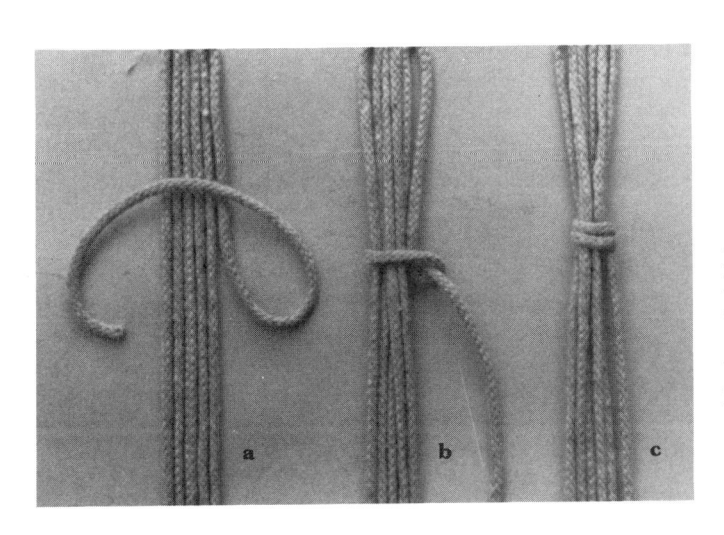

Illus. 28. **Formation of two Collecting Knots.** *a:* Form a loop with a side cord and bring it over as shown; *b:* Bring the end under the group of cords and out through the loop and pull tightly in place; *c:* Repeat to form two Collecting Knots.

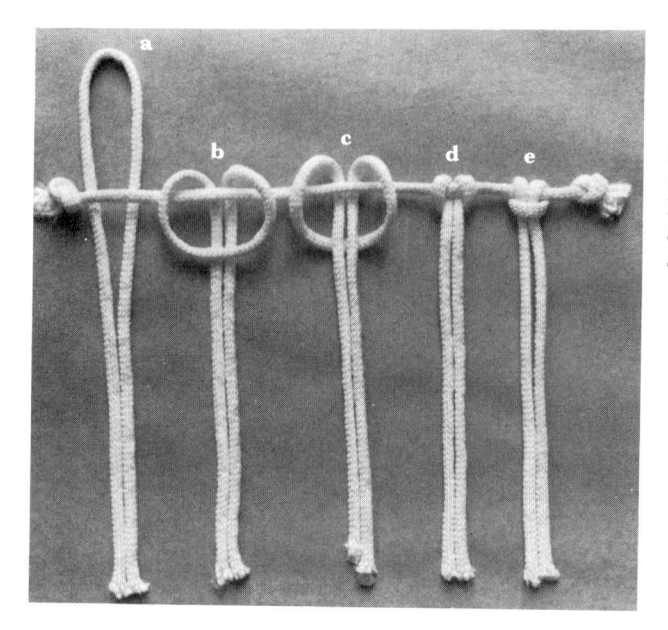

Illus. 29. Formation of Lark's Head Knot.
a: **Place the loop under the foundation Knot Bearer;** *b:* **Fold this loop over the two cords;** *c:* **Take the two cords through the loop;** *d:* **Pull the ends downwards, tightly;** *e:* **Reverse side of d.**

Lark's Head Knot

The Lark's Head Knot is usually made to mount cords on a base which may be either another piece of cord or a dowel. It is also useful for rug-hooking (discussed on page 38). To make this knot, follow Illus. 29.

a: Place a loop under the KB.
b: Fold this loop (open) forwards over the KB and the two cords.
c: Take the two cords through the loop.
d: Pull the ends tight and let the cords hang downwards.
e: The reverse of this knot.

Buttonhole Knot

To make a Single Buttonhole Knot, follow Illus. 30.

a: Bring the WT over and around the KB, then out through the space between the two cords.

b-c: Repeat this to make a sennit of Single Buttonhole Knots. Notice in Illus. 30c how the sennit automatically twists.

Illus. 31 shows a chain of Single Buttonhole Knots. To make a chain like this one, alternately knot the WT and the KB into Single Buttonhole Knots.

To make Double Buttonhole Knots, follow Illus. 32.

a: First make one Single Buttonhole Knot, and then reverse it . . . bring the WT under and around, and out through the space between the two cords; pull the end to bring the second twisting close to the first to complete the knot.

b: A sennit of Double Buttonhole Knots.
c: Alternate Double Buttonhole Knots, using three cords.

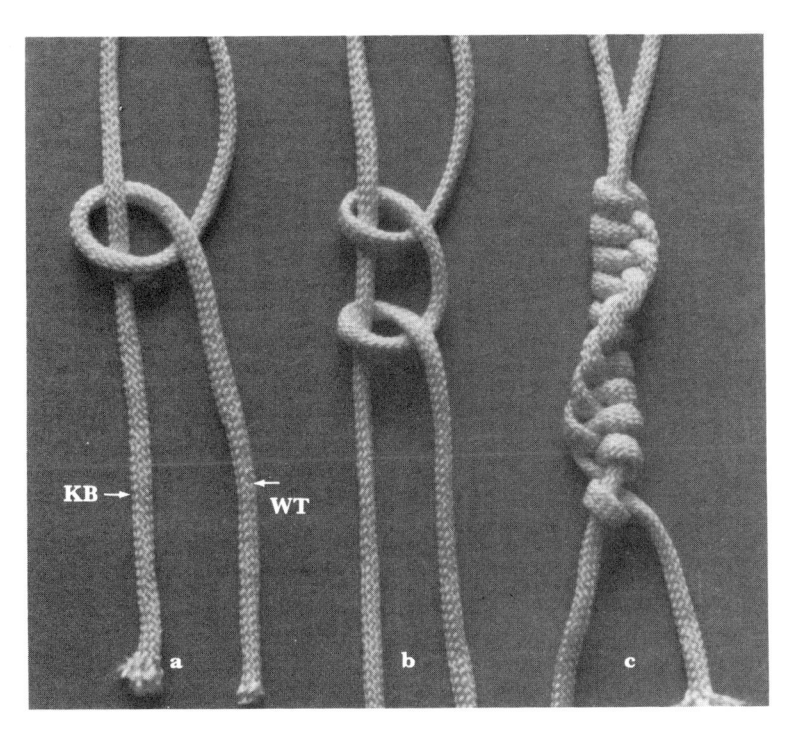

Illus. 30. Formation of a Single Buttonhole Knot. *a:* Bring the Working Thread over and around the Knot Bearer, then out through the space between the two cords; *b:* Repeat this to make a sennit of Single Buttonhole Knots; *c:* A sennit of Single Buttonhole Knots.

Illus. 31. A chain of Single Buttonhole Knots.

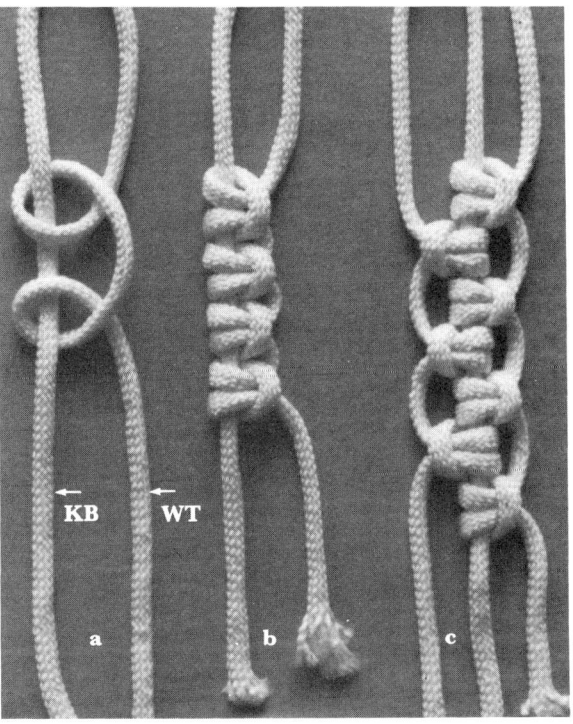

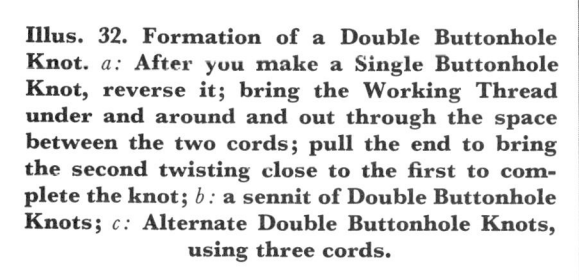

Illus. 32. Formation of a Double Buttonhole Knot. *a:* After you make a Single Buttonhole Knot, reverse it; bring the Working Thread under and around and out through the space between the two cords; pull the end to bring the second twisting close to the first to complete the knot; *b:* a sennit of Double Buttonhole Knots; *c:* Alternate Double Buttonhole Knots, using three cords.

Design and Color

Once you have mastered the basic macramé knots, there is no limit to the variety of combinations or patterns that you can create. The more freely you design, the more interesting your results will be. Try to cultivate a constant and sensitive awareness of the designs your environment offers. Forms and patterns found in nature offer an endless source of ideas for macramé. Look at flowers, leaves, tree barks, roots, cellular patterns in vegetable and animal matter—these are just a few natural designs which can serve as rich inspirations for many projects. Other works of art, historic or contemporary, can stir your imagination as well. Architectural structures suggest geometric forms and shapes. Primitive sculptures and artifacts are also very good visual sources.

Most living organisms are relatively symmetrical and well-balanced, but your creative fabric project may very well take on an unbalanced design. You are totally free to interpret Nature in any way you choose. At times, you may create a purely realistic design, at others, expressionistic forms without any resemblance at all to an existing object.

Color plays a very important rôle in designing. In macramé, particularly, you can achieve numerous color effects because the cords often change places and it is only the Working Thread that carries the color which appears on the surface of a knotted work. Observe the interplay of colors in the macramé work in Illus. 22 and 23.

Choose the colors for your projects by keeping in mind the mood you intend to convey, as well as the personality and taste of the person for whom you are creating the piece. You may choose cool colors (blues and greens) to convey a feeling of calmness, tranquility or sadness, or warm colors (reds and yellows) to convey a feeling of excitement, cheerfulness or happiness. Also decide whether to use an intense or subtle combination of colors—that is, complementary, monochromatic (different shades of one color) or related color schemes. You can test the effect you will achieve by placing different skeins of yarns together to determine how well they go together, before beginning to work on the project. Experience often helps train your eye to judge color combinations, but you can use a color wheel to help if you are a beginner.

Finishing

How you finish your macramé project is almost as important as which knots you made and which designs and colors you combined. You can ruin the entire effect of any piece with a sloppy finishing job.

There are various ways in which you can finish off your work. A frequently used method is to leave the cord-ends hanging loosely to form fringes. You can also bunch the cord-ends together by tying or wrapping them neatly. Sometimes, you might want to fray these ends further by unravelling the plies of the cords. In the pieces by Irmari Nacht shown in Illus. 33 and 66, this finish was used very

Illus. 33. Macramé and rug-hooking, as well as fraying the cord-ends to give a curly-hair effect, comprise this unique wall hanging by Irmari Nacht.

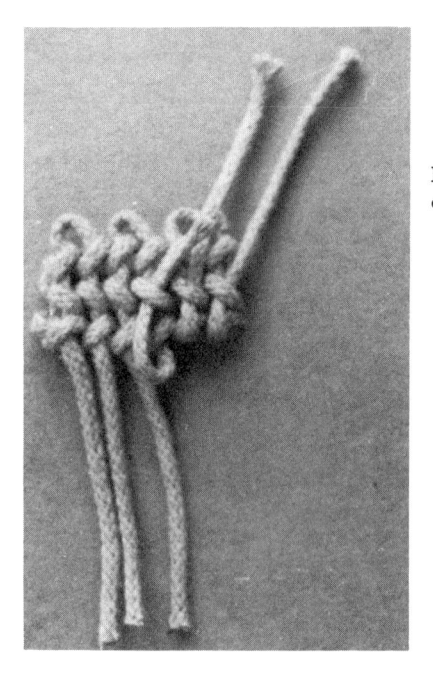

Illus. 34. If you want a neatly finished edge without hanging ends, tuck the cord-ends in behind each knot by using a large-eyed needle or crochet hook.

effectively. You can also trim loose ends to whatever lengths you choose, or add on more filler fibres and then wrap them to give a tassel- or pile-look (an example of this is shown in Illus. B3).

Sometimes, you might want to use materials other than just the cords to finish your work. Feathers, for example, are interesting when wrapped together with the cord-ends. Illus. C3 and D2 show examples of this.

For another finishing touch, insert beads into each cord-end as was done in Illus. 118 and 120. Alternately, you can work Bead Knots (see Illus. 27) on each cord to simulate beads.

Occasionally, you might prefer a neat edge without hanging ends. In this case, tuck the cord-ends in behind each knot, using a large-eyed needle or crochet hook, as shown in Illus. 34. Glue these ends on the back side to keep them secure.

Now that you are familiar with the macramé technique, you are ready to think even more creatively and to consider combining the basic knots with other textile crafts you know. Here are seven chapters of ideas to inspire you. Each one discusses specific techniques and media and gives step-by-step instructions for the projects in this book. You can, if you want, copy the items pictured and described or you can—and this is much more interesting—simply use these directions as a springboard to making original, and inevitably more satisfying creations. Experiment and invent! There is no end to the fun you can have nor to the things you can make.

Part II: Macramé Plus

Macramé Plus Wrapping and Coiling

WRAPPING

Knotters frequently use wrapping to bundle cord-ends together to provide a neat finish. At any point, you can wrap groups of Working Threads either to form an integral part of your design or simply to enhance your macramé piece. Wrapping allows you to introduce a new color, texture or dimension. You can also

Illus. 35. This circular wall hanging by Irmari Nacht is entitled "Africa." The macramé and wrapping, made from jute cord and electric wire, were mounted on a bicycle hoop.

Illus. 36. This close-up shows how to bundle loose cords using the wrapping technique.

Illus. 37 (left). You can make a neat finish by tucking the wrapping fibre-end beneath the wrapped core with the aid of a large-eyed needle. Then cut off the end.

Illus. 38 (right). This unusually shaped hanging, which combines macramé, weaving, wrapping, stuffing and rug-hooking (using Lark's Head Knots), was made from light and heavy wool rug yarns. Shredded foam stuffed the hand-woven fabric which serves as the background for the root-like structures made from macramé and wrapped cord-ends. Illus. 73 shows a close-up.

use it to create a new shape in a sculptured form. In fact, you can use wrapping, as many artist-craftspeople have, either alone or in conjunction with other textile techniques to create enormous wall hangings, room dividers or other monumental constructions.

Wrapping is what its name implies. To do it, you wrap lengths of fibres, single or multiple lengths, around multiples of other fibres (called fillers or cores), in whatever thickness you choose. Firm or tightly-spun cords, such as twines, ropes or braided cords of various weights or thicknesses, and even metal wires or wood rods, may serve as cores for wrapping.

You can use various sizes, textures and colors of threads, as long as they are pliable enough to wrap round the core. Silk, jute, wool, cotton and synthetic yarns are all good for wrapping. In Illus. A1, for instance, hand-spun wool, cotton, camel and goat hair, together with commercial rug yarns, were used for the wrapping and macramé areas.

It is important that you secure the wrapping fibre-ends well. When you are using a rather rough-textured wrapping fibre, it is sometimes sufficient to end the wrapping with two Collecting Knots (see Illus. 28). Otherwise, use a dab of fabric glue to keep it well in place. You can achieve a neater finish by tucking the wrapping fibre-end well beneath the wrapped fibres by using a large-eyed needle (see Illus. 37). Then cut off the end.

Depending on how you wrap, you can produce intriguing effects. If you wrap the fibres tightly enough, your wrapped structure can stand up without your

Illus. 39. Wool rug yarns were knotted and wrapped tightly to make this unusual self-supporting weed pot. Shells were glued on at the bumps.

having to use wire, wood or metal frames. Illus. 39 is an example of this. To achieve this firmness, push the wrapping fibres together with your thumb and forefinger as you wrap the entire core length.

You can then stitch together wrapped cores, as was done to create the arch from the wrapped sisal twines in Illus. 67 (shown close-up in Illus. 40). To vary the thickness of the wrapped area, either add on new short pieces of filler fibres,

Illus. 40. This close-up of Illus. 67 is a good example of wrapped sisal twines stitched together to form an arched structure.

Illus. 41. This close-up of Illus. C2 shows wrapped cores mixed with macramé and hooked yarns. Note the special effect created by the variations in the thicknesses of the wrapped cores.

Illus. 42. In this sculptured creation, the macramé cords were periodically wrapped, and then the macramé was resumed. As in Illus. 41, note the artistic effect created by variations in the thicknesses of the wrapped cords.

gradually increasing the thickness, or re-wrap the core over, several times, until you have obtained the desired thickness. Neatly wrap over the ends of these additions with the final wrapping fibre (see Illus. 41 and 42).

Try wrapping other objects such as feathers, twigs or straw into the piece. Illus. 43 is an example of feathers added to wrapped ends.

For another method of wrapping fibre-ends, see Illus. 44 (this technique was used in the neck piece in Illus. A3). The wrapping was first made into a loop at about the distance of the planned wrapping length. The wrapping was then made from

Illus. 43. This close-up of color Illus. D2 is an example of feathers added to wrapped ends. You can add any objects you choose to uniquely finish off wrapped off ends.

Illus. 44. For this method of wrapping, first make a loop as shown on the left. Wrap around the core, inserting the end through the loop when you reach the bottom. Then push the whole wrapping down in place.

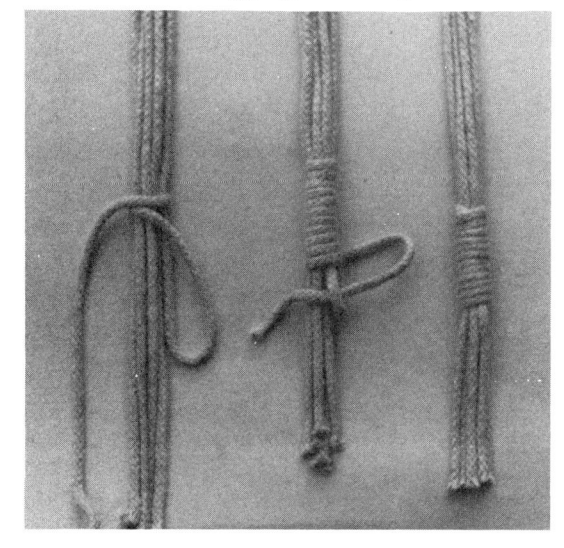

the starting point, round the core. The end was inserted through the loop. Finally, the whole wrapping was pushed down tightly in place.

The examples of wrapping in this book show how versatile this technique can be when you use it in combination with macramé and other textile crafts. Remember, of course, that you do not have to copy the projects pictured here, but you should feel free to experiment with techniques and designs you create. As a guide, however, you might be interested in the following instructions for making the unusual weed pot in Illus. 39, using both macramé and the wrapping technique.

Weed Pot

Materials
rug yarn in two colors: first color: light grey; second color: dark grey
Money Cowrie shells

Step 1: Start at the top with 12 Flat Knots (FK) (a total of 48 strands), which you anchor to a working base with pins. Then join them into a circular formation with a row of Double Knots (DK). Use a separate strand as the Knot Bearer (KB).

Step 2: Make another row of 12 FKs.

Step 3: Make a sennit of 4 FKs between 3 FKs (see Illus. 45).

Step 4: Working in groups of 4 (12 strands each), make a left Diagonal and a right Diagonal DK Bar, starting from the middle FK (see Illus. 47).

Step 5: Make 4 more successive left and right Diagonal DK Bars, using a new KB of the second color with each bar, thus introducing the second color. See Illus. 22 for how to introduce the fifth colored strand.

Step 6: Use all the second color strands to construct rose buds to join groups of DK Bars together. Make a rose bud as follows: with 8 strands, using cord #5 as KB (see Illus. 46a), make a left Diagonal DK Bar; with cord #4 as KB, make a right Diagonal DK Bar (see Illus. 46b). Make 2 more successive Diagonals with open ends (see Illus. 46c). Then reverse the Diagonals (see Illus. 46c to 46e). Push

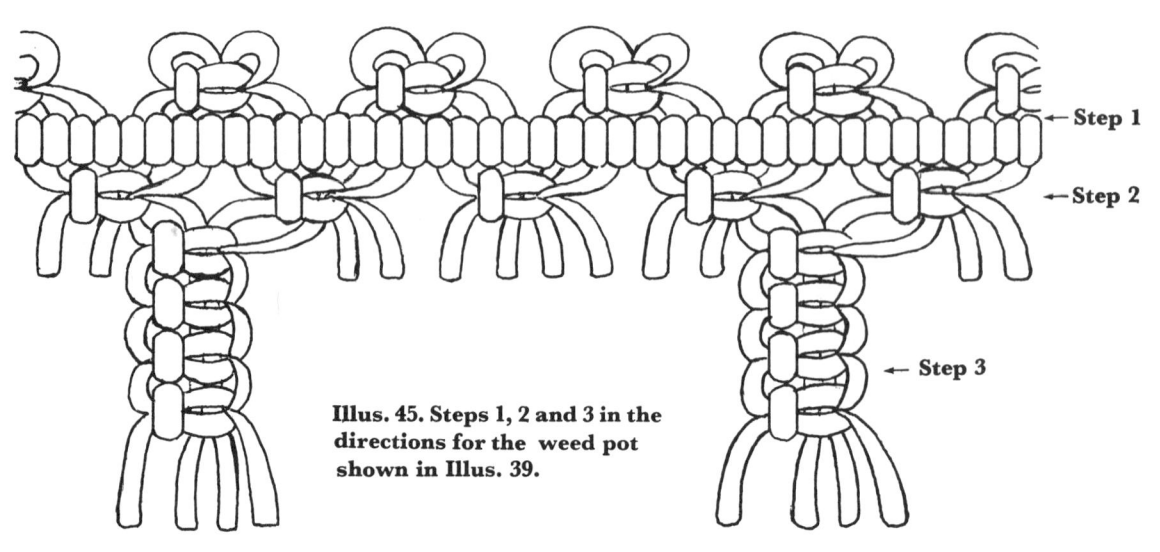

Illus. 45. Steps 1, 2 and 3 in the directions for the weed pot shown in Illus. 39.

Illus. 46a.

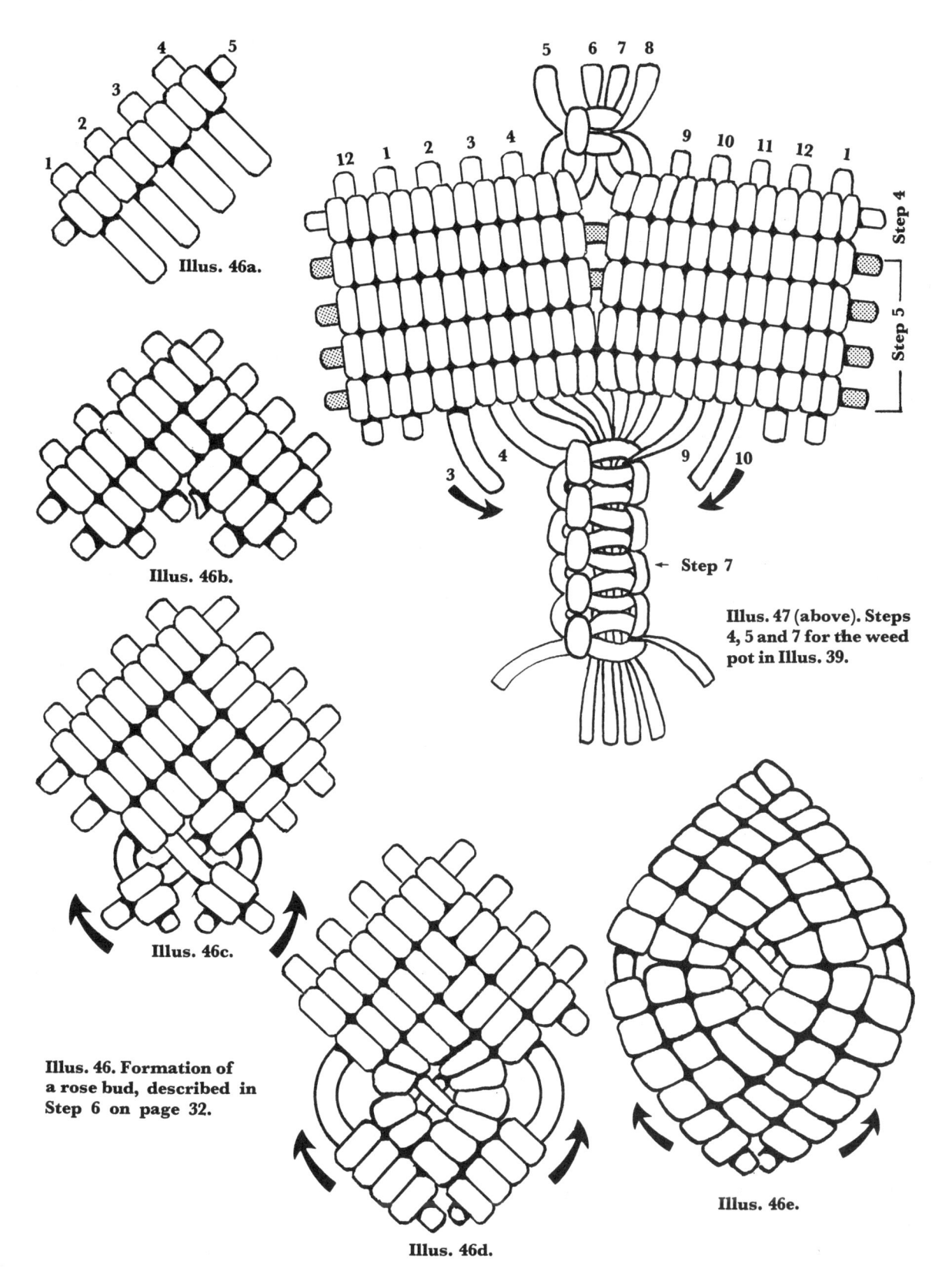

Illus. 46b.

Illus. 46c.

Illus. 46. Formation of a rose bud, described in Step 6 on page 32.

Illus. 46d.

Illus. 46e.

Illus. 47 (above). Steps 4, 5 and 7 for the weed pot in Illus. 39.

33

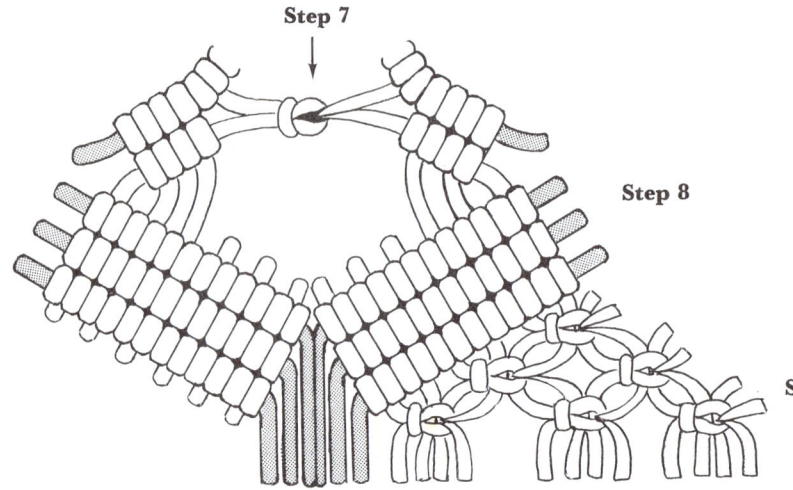

Illus. 48. Steps 7, 8 and 9 in the directions for the weed pot in Illus. 39. The Flat Knot sennit you made in Step 7 lies over the Square Knot.

the DKs on each bar up close to each other in order to raise the entire structure, before joining the left to the right Diagonal Bar with another DK.

Step 7: Going back to the first color, using cords #4 and #9 as WTs, make a sennit of 5 FKs at the middle (see Illus. 47). Make an SK using cords #3 and #10,

Illus. 49 (above). You can create an exciting contrast in texture by placing wrapping done with smooth yarn right next to wrapping done with rough, hand-spun cotton yarn, as is shown here.

Illus. 50 (left). Here, neatly wrapped cord-ends and the macramé area are surrounded by contrasting wrapping done with hand-spun yarns.

Illus. 51. An example of figure eight coiling.

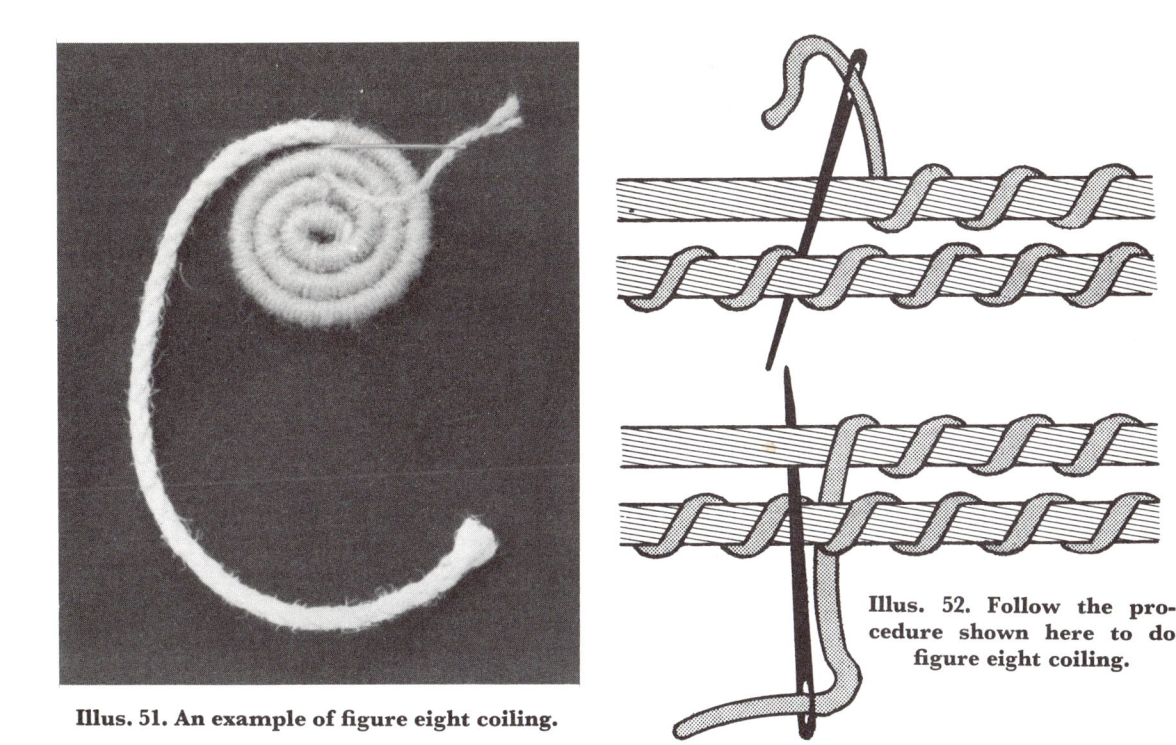

Illus. 52. Follow the procedure shown here to do figure eight coiling.

to lift the sennit over into a bridge-like structure. Then make a left and right DK Bar just below the last bars (see Illus. 48).

Step 8: Make 2 or 3 more left and right DK Bars, using the second color strands as KBs.

Step 9: Use a network of FKs to fill in the bottom spaces (see Illus. 48).

Step 10: Divide the remaining length of strands into 8 equal groups and then wrap tightly with a second color strand, in order to form the standing arms. See Illus. 37 for the wrapping method.

If you want, you can glue Money Cowrie shells on the surface of the sennits, using glue or cement. Sew a circular, crocheted piece, made from the same yarn, to the bottom of the pot for support.

Add dried flowers, if you wish, to complete your weed pot.

COILING

Coiling is a form of wrapping. You wrap and join together the wrapped elements as you make a coil. Coiling is very useful for making baskets or containers, as it provides an easy means of working in any shape you want. Two simple methods of coiling are illustrated here. One method of coiling is called figure eight (8) coiling; follow Illus. 51 and 52. If you plan to wrap in the direction towards you, bring the wrapping fibre-end under the core, then behind the previous wrapped coil. Now, with the aid of a needle, pass the wrapping end through to the front side, and back again between the two coils, thereby wrapping round the previous coil. Continue the wrapping on the top coil and the figure eight is completed. Repeat this process at intervals of about half an inch.

Illus. 53 (left). Another method of coiling is called lace stitch coiling. Follow the directions on page 37 and the diagram in Illus. 54 to do this technique.

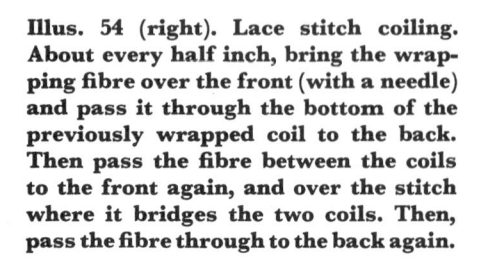

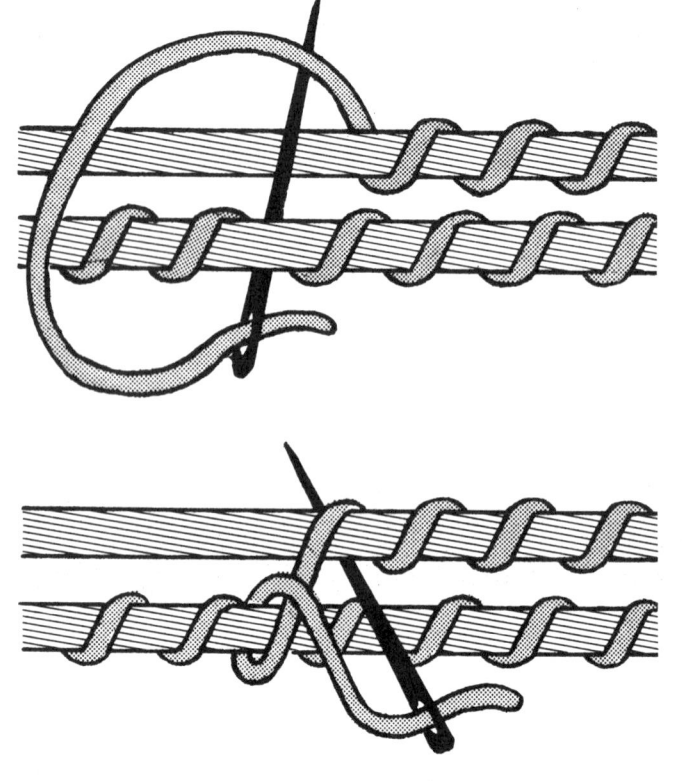

Illus. 54 (right). Lace stitch coiling. About every half inch, bring the wrapping fibre over the front (with a needle) and pass it through the bottom of the previously wrapped coil to the back. Then pass the fibre between the coils to the front again, and over the stitch where it bridges the two coils. Then, pass the fibre through to the back again.

Illus. 55 (above). This coiled basket, made of nubby cotton-rayon yarn, is decorated with macramé made of primitive spun wool.

Illus. 56 (right). Another view of the coiled basket in Illus. 55.

Another method of coiling is called lace stitch coiling. Follow Illus. 53 and 54. Bring the wrapping fibre over the front and pass it through the bottom of the previously wrapped coil, with the aid of a needle, to the back side. Then pass it between the coils to the front side again, and over across the stitch where it bridges the two coils. Finally, pass it through to the back side once more. Continue the wrapping, repeating the lace stitch at intervals of about half an inch.

Illus. 55 and 56 show two views of a coiled basket, with macramé.

Macramé Plus Rug-Hooking

Rug-hooking is a natural craft to combine with macramé. Lark's Head Knots (see Illus. 29 on page 22), the most common macramé knots used in combining these two techniques, form the hooked effect. What you do to create the rug pile is knot Lark's Head Knots, from cut rug yarns, onto a net-like structure, usually made up of either Bead Knots, as shown in Illus. 58, or Flat Knots (see the top section of Illus. 12). (The back side of the hanging in Illus. B3 is shown close-up in Illus. 57, where Lark's Head Knots were made on a network of Flat Knots, which serve as the foundation for the rug-hooking.)

You can also use Lark's Head Knots when hooking cut pile onto crocheted or knitted areas which you have combined with macramé. When hooking onto a knitted piece, knot the pile round two threads of the foundation, because of the nature of the knitted stitches. Use a crochet hook to make it easier to insert the loop onto the foundation when you form the Lark's Head Knot.

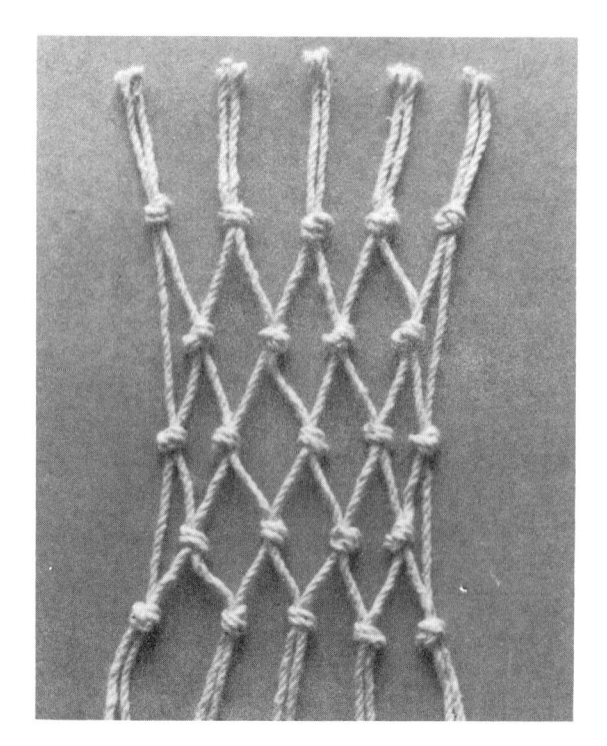

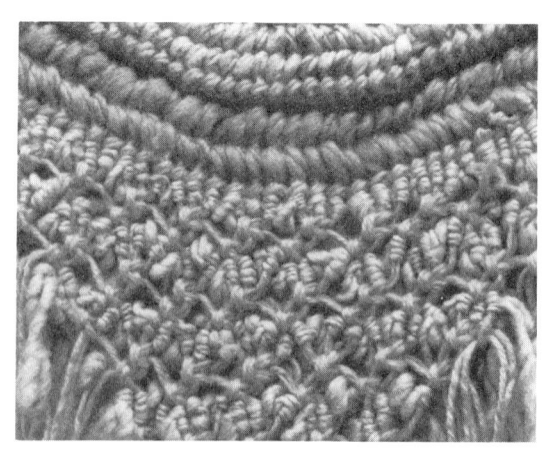

Illus. 57. This close-up of the underside of Illus. B3 illustrates Lark's Head Knots worked on a net-like structure made of Flat Knots.

Illus. 58 (left). Another way you can combine macramé and rug-hooking is to make Lark's Head Knots on a network of Bead Knots, as shown here. You work the Lark's Head Knots on the floating cords between the Bead Knots.

Illus. 59 (left). In this close-up view of color Illus. C2, you can see that yarn was hooked onto the woven background. Also notice the striking textured effect achieved by surrounding the macramé area in the middle with wrapping.

Illus. 60 (right). Another attractive method of combining macramé and rug-hooking is to make Ghiordes Knots, as shown here, using the floating strands of the macramé as the foundation.

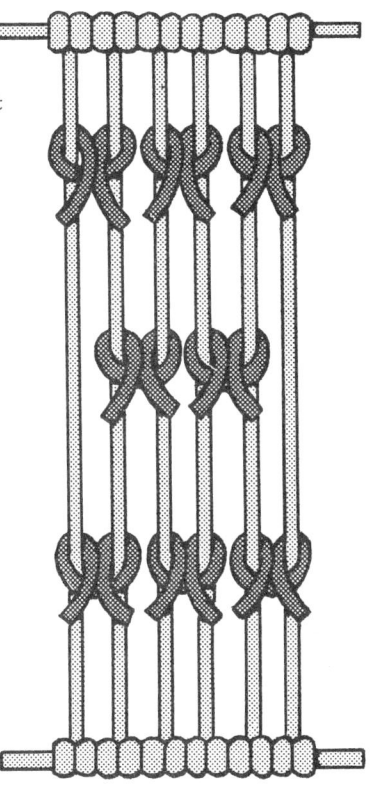

In the wall hanging in Illus. C1, the pile was hooked, using this method, onto the knitted area in the middle. You can, likewise, use this method to hook onto a piece of weaving (see Illus. C2 and the close-up in Illus. 59).

The formation of Ghiordes Knots is another method which you can use as the foundation for rug-type knots in the areas of floating strands in a macramé piece. Use the floating strands as the foundation for knotting the cut yarns (see Illus. 60). In Illus. 61, sisal pile was knotted between two Horizontal DK Bars on the floating cords.

1. An effective use of Ghiordes Knots is shown here. Sisal was knotted on the floating cords between two Horizontal Double Knot Bars.

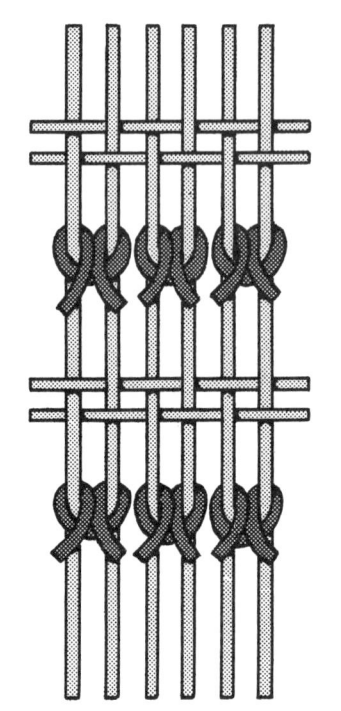

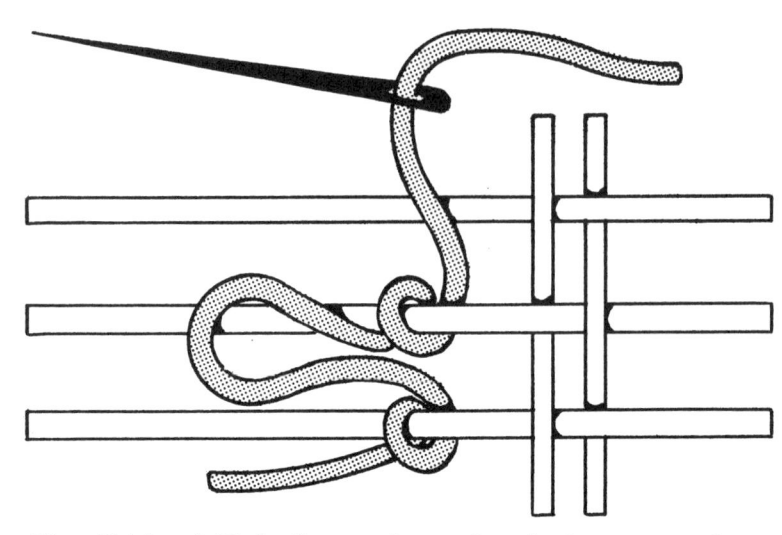

Illus. 63 (above). To hook a continuous length of yarn, use a large-eyed needle as shown.

Illus. 62 (left). As you can see here, you can also work Ghiordes Knots using the warp threads between the wefts on a woven piece as the foundation.

You may also work Ghiordes Knots in-between rows of wefts, or groups of wefts, in a woven area. (Illus. 62 shows how to do this.)

If you plan to hook a continuous length of yarn on any foundation, use a large-eyed needle. Wrap the yarn around the foundation thread, as shown in Illus. 63, at the same time you secure the pile in place. You can also use a ruler to keep a uniform pile length by catching the loops on it. You can leave the loops thus formed as they are, as was done in Illus. G2, or you may clip them later to form a cut pile.

The simplest method of forming looped pile is to hold the continuous length of yarn on the underside of the foundation, and, by means of a crochet hook, to draw the loops through to the top side, to the desired lengths (see Illus. 64). How-

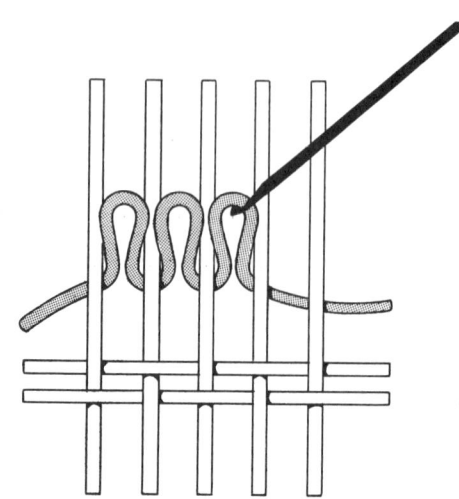

Illus. 64. The simplest way to form looped pile is pictured here. Hold the continuous length of yarn or fibre under the foundation, and draw loops through to the top side using a crochet hook. Since this method does not secure the pile well, however, you have to brush a rubber or latex adhesive on the back of the foundation to hold the loops in place.

Illus. 65. In this close-up of color Illus. C3, the pile was created in the woven area using the method pictured in Illus. 64. You can leave the loops uncut, as was done here, or cut them for a different effect. The contrasting texture of the macramé sennits knotted from the warp threads adds special interest.

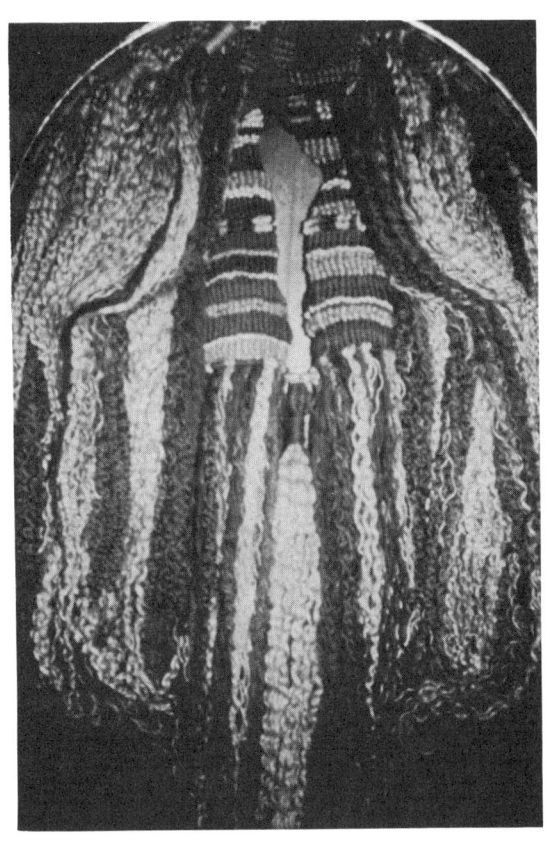

Illus. 66. This wild-looking wall hanging by Irmari Nacht combines macramé and rug-hooking. The cord-ends were frayed to achieve the rich, kinky pile effect which characterizes the creation. The hanging was mounted on a bicycle hoop.

ever, this does not secure the pile well, especially if you are using evenly textured or smooth yarns. You must brush a rubber or latex adhesive, which is available from rug-hooking supply shops, on the back side of the foundation after you have completed all the hooking. In Illus. 65, a close-up of Illus. C3, the pile was hooked on the woven area using this method and loops were left uncut. The distances between the hooked or knotted pile are determined by the weight or thickness of the yarn you use.

To obtain a more interesting texture on the finished surface, you can cut the pile yarns at different lengths or heights. Your result will be multi-levelled areas. If you also use exotic yarns that are highly textured, you can create a striking tactile surface on your hooked creations. Take a look at Illus. 33 and 66 to see a few of the kinds of effects you can create by combining hooking and macramé.

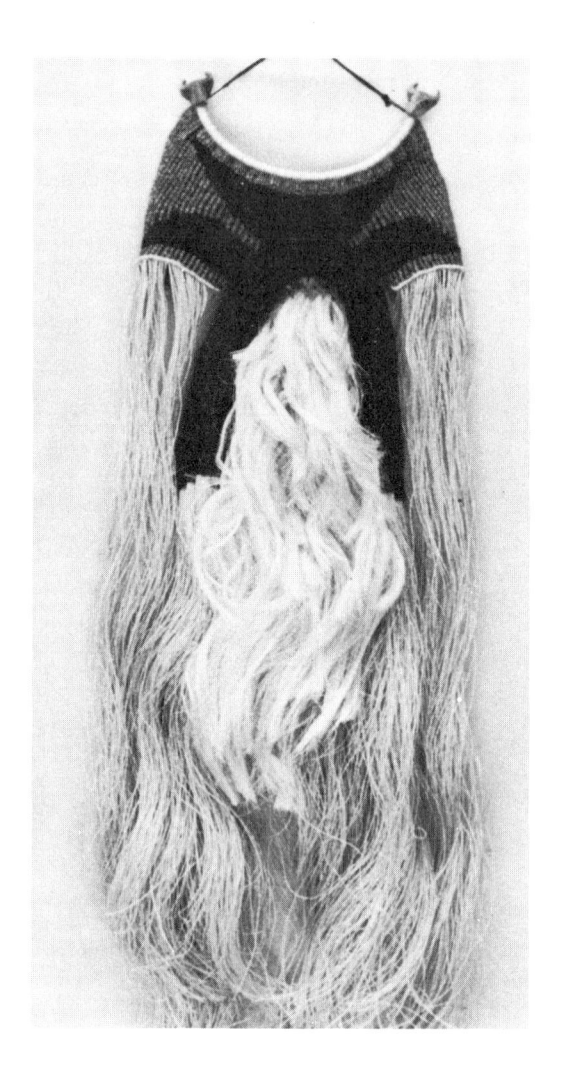

Illus. 67 (left). Natural sisal and synthetic yarns created this striking wall hanging, whose directions begin below. The top area of the hanging was made entirely of Double Knots; the arched shape in the middle was formed by stitching together wrapped twines. Sisal was knotted between the arch, using Lark's Head Knots, onto a foundation of Bead Knots. Bamboo with carved wooden buffalo heads was used as a dowel.

Illus. 68 (below). How to knot rows of Vertical Double Knots using a single strand as the Working Thread.

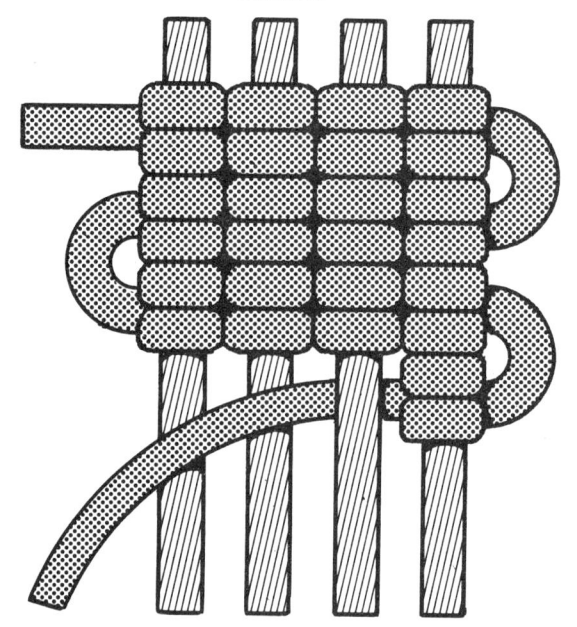

WALL HANGING

For a simple project in which rug-hooking was combined with wrapping and macramé, see Illus. 67. The twines were mounted on bamboo dowel. The whole piece was worked in double strands instead of the usual single strand. Follow the instructions below to make the 22 inch × 6½ foot hanging pictured, or adapt them to create an original hanging using these techniques.

Materials
natural fine sisal twines
polyester yarns in two different colors

  Step 1: Mount 60 loops of double strands of twine by Lark's Head Knots.
  Step 2: Work the first color strands of polyester yarn into Vertical DK Bars for

about $\frac{3}{4}$ inch (see Illus. 68 for knotting Vertical DK Bars using a single strand as the Working Thread).

Step 3: Working in Vertical DK Bars, but this time over each 2 double strands of twine as KBs, introduce the second color strands into the areas shown in the design in Illus. 69, leaving an arched shape at the middle. Complete each side panel and finish off with a row of DK Bars.

Step 4: Make the first wrapped element (to form the arched shape) by using a half-inch thickness of twines as a core. Start the wrapping from the middle of the length (at the top of the arch) and work downwards. As the wrapping progresses, take some free twines from the arched area into the core in order to set it in place (see Illus. 37 for the wrapping method).

Step 5: Now make 5 separate wrapped cores and stitch them together to the first arched element.

Step 6: At the middle arched area, knot the free twines into a network of Bead Knots, as shown in Illus. 58.

Step 7: Knot lengths of cut sisal fibre on the sides of each Bead Knot, using Lark's Head Knots (see Illus. 29).

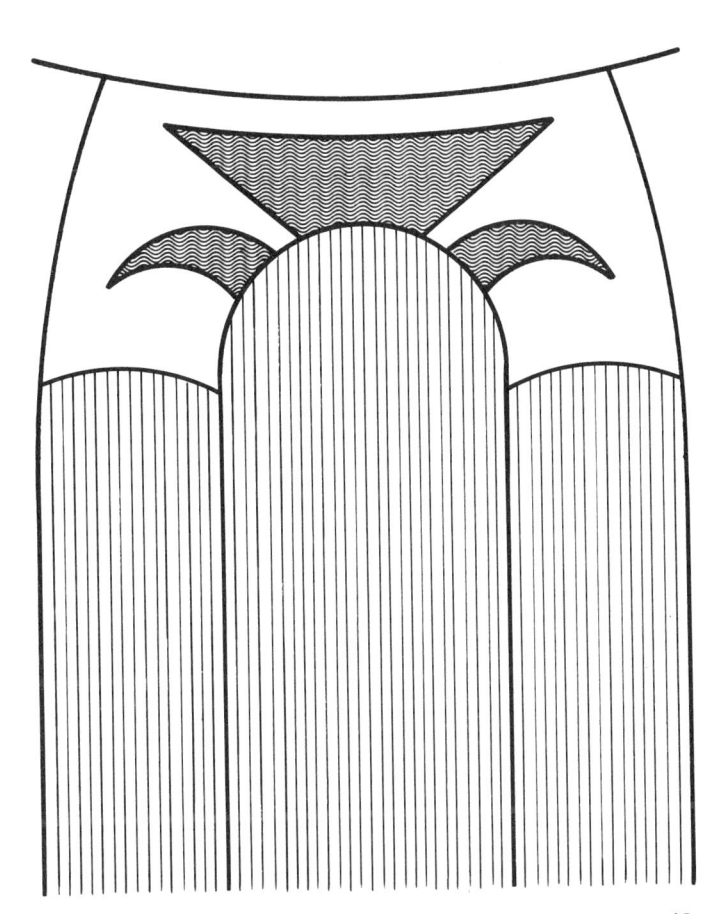

Illus. 69. Pattern for the various sections of the design in Illus. 67.

Macramé Plus Weaving

Weaving is another craft which combines naturally with macramé. You can incorporate a woven section into your macramé as supplementary decoration or use it as an integral part of the overall construction or design. By incorporating areas of weaving into your knotted structures, or vice versa, you create exciting contrasts in surface textures. Illus. 71 and the close-up in Illus. 70 are examples of macramé combined with weaving.

Weaving is the process of interlacing horizontal threads, called wefts, under

Illus. 70 (above). The raised macramé area in this close-up of the hanging in Illus. 71 adds dimension as well as contrast in color to the plain or tabby weaving.

Illus. 71 (left). A cardboard loom was used to create this handsome wall hanging in which wool rug yarn, fleece and synthetic yarn were used to do the macramé and plain weaving. Additional pile was knotted on at the bottom and sides.

Illus. 72. In plain or tabby weave, pictured here, the vertical warp and horizontal weft threads are visible on the finished surface.

Illus. 73. Macramé cord-ends wrapped and tucked into a woven base resulted in this interestingly textured portion of a fibre art composition.

and over the vertically arranged threads called warps. The two simple weaves most often used in combination with macramé are the plain or tabby weave, and the tapestry weave. In plain weave, the warp and weft threads are both visible on the finished surface of the weave (see Illus. 72), while in tapestry weave, the weft threads entirely cover the warp threads, so that only the weft threads are visible on the finished surface (see Illus. 74). Illus. 75 shows a mixture of plain and tapestry weaves.

In combining weaving with macramé, you do not need to be concerned with the complex patterns a weaver usually works with. Keep your approach quite simple. Visualize your project in terms of form and shape, color and texture, rather than focussing in on the intricate designs possible in weaving. If you are an experienced and adept weaver, you can, of course, use a conventional loom. Otherwise, weave by means of the simplest devices available, which can even be as primitive as using your own fingers (finger weaving) or a needle (needle weaving), or other non-loom equipment that you can easily construct at home. Non-loom weaving means simple weaving without the use of the conventional wood loom equipped with heddles,

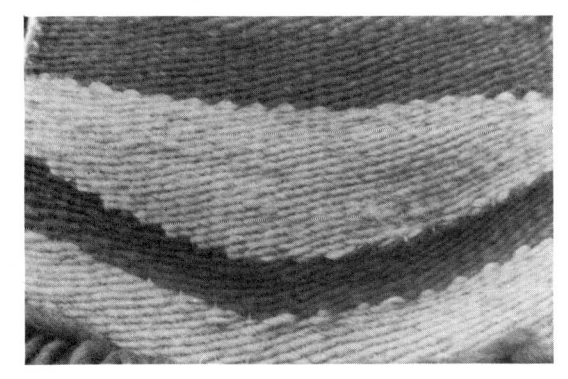

Illus. 74. In tapestry weave, pictured here, only the horizontal weft threads are visible on the woven surface.

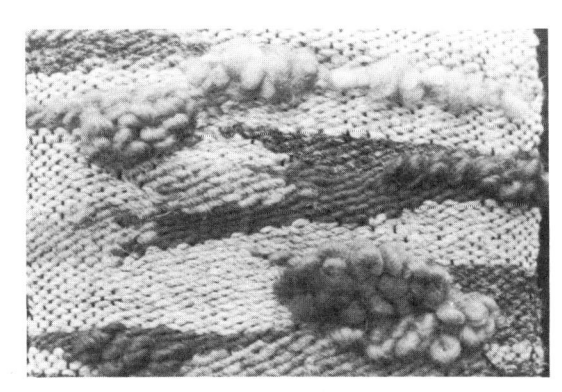

Illus. 75. This woven sample combines plain and tapestry weaves, as well as some wool fleece for textural diversion.

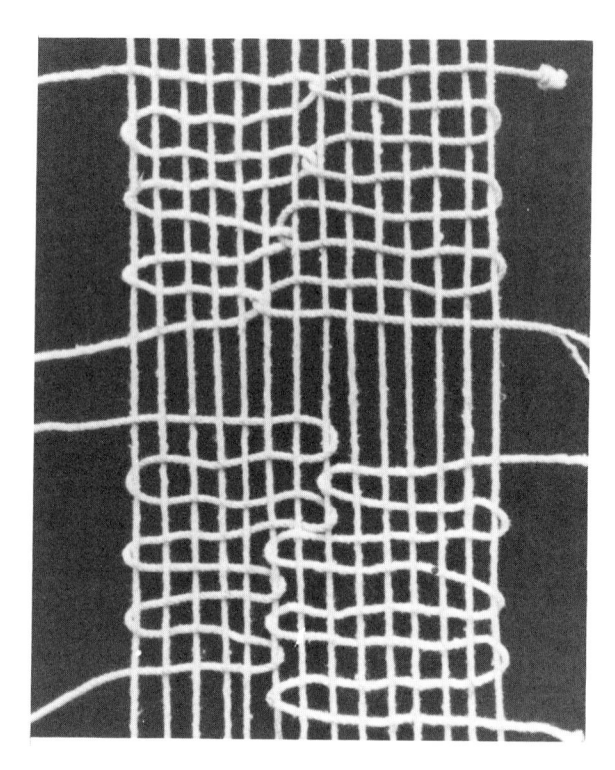

Illus. 77 (above). The woven areas in this close-up of color Illus. E1 consist of floating macramé cords used as warp threads. The tapestry weaving was done with a needle after all the macramé was completed.

Illus. 76 (left). To change threads in weaving—for color or texture—use either an interlocking (see the top section) or dove-tailing (see the bottom section) method.

beaters or pedals that is used by experts or industrial weavers. These methods are less restrictive than loom methods and you can more easily create a variety of improvised structures. They also facilitate experimentation with different materials

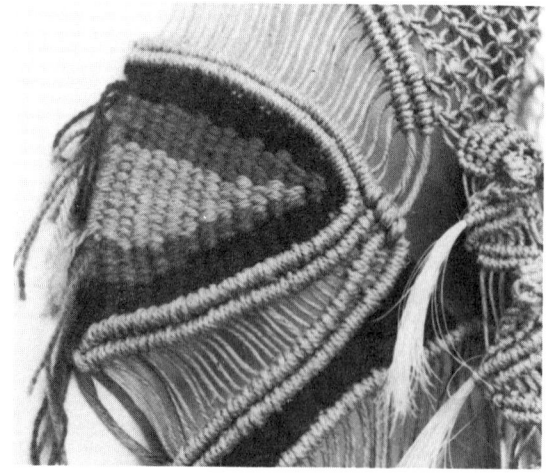

Illus. 78. Note, in this close-up photograph of color Illus. B2, some of the floating macramé cords were left alone, while others were used as warp threads for needle tapestry weaving. Double Knot Bars emphasize shapes in the design.

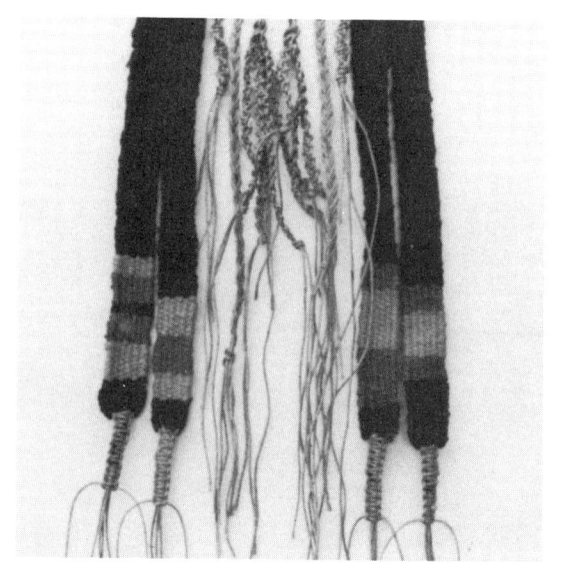

Illus. 79. This close-up of another part of color Illus. B2 features woven strips, using macramé cords as the warp threads.

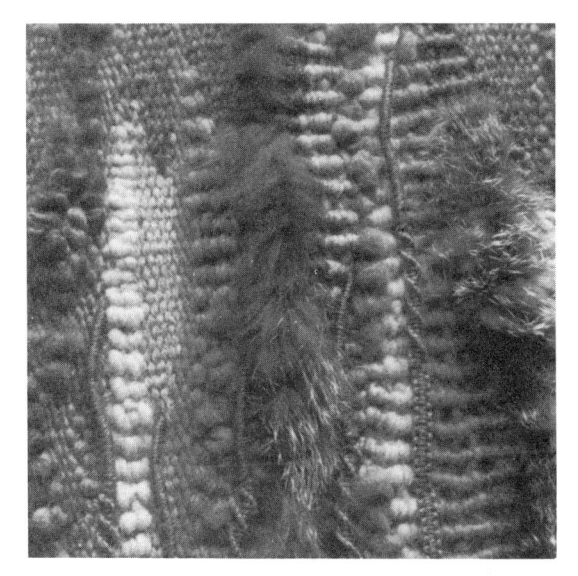

Illus. 80. In this close-up of color Illus. D3, you can see the results of using the warp threads of a woven area as macramé cords. Here, Vertical Double Knot Bars were made between the weft threads. The warp threads were used as Knot Bearers.

Illus. 81. Flat Knot sennits were folded over to form graceful loops in this close-up of one of the dolls in color Illus. E2. Further texture was created by weaving mohair into the floating macramé cords.

and the formation of different shapes, because they leave you a wide range of movement and you are free to depart from traditional weaving techniques. You may weave loosely or tightly. As a beater, simply use your fingers, a comb, a fork or even a flat stick. You may choose to distort the sides or edges of the woven fabric by controlling the tension of the weft threads.

To change threads, colors or textures, you can use an interlocking or dove-tailing method. Illus. 76 pictures both techniques.

When combining weaving with macramé, the vertical cords used in knotting become warp threads for weaving (see Illus. 77, 78 and 79). On the other hand, you may use warp threads in weaving as macramé cords, as was done, for example, in Illus. 1, 80 and 81. Some knotters use the cords in macramé work to weave a diamond area between rows of knots (see Illus. 82).

Illus. 82. You can create striking effects by introducing differently shaped sections into your work. One way to do this is to weave a diamond-shaped area between rows of Double Knots, as shown here.

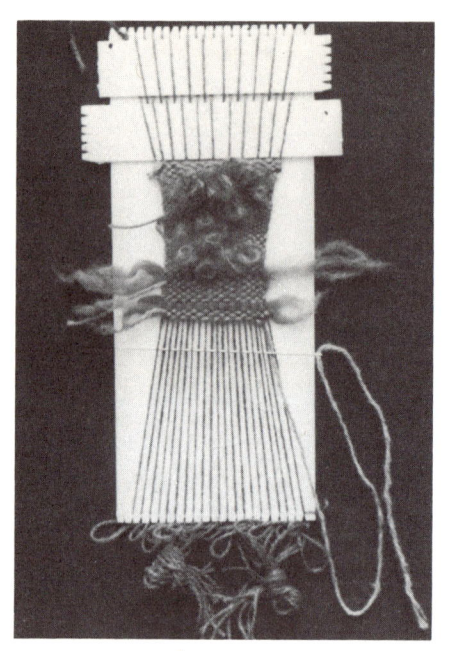

Illus. 83. One type of loom you can easily construct is a cardboard loom like the one shown here. Knot pre-cut lengths of warp threads at the bottom notches to use in the macramé work after you complete the weaving. Do not hesitate to experiment with different yarn textures. Here, looped mohair threads are being inserted between the weft threads.

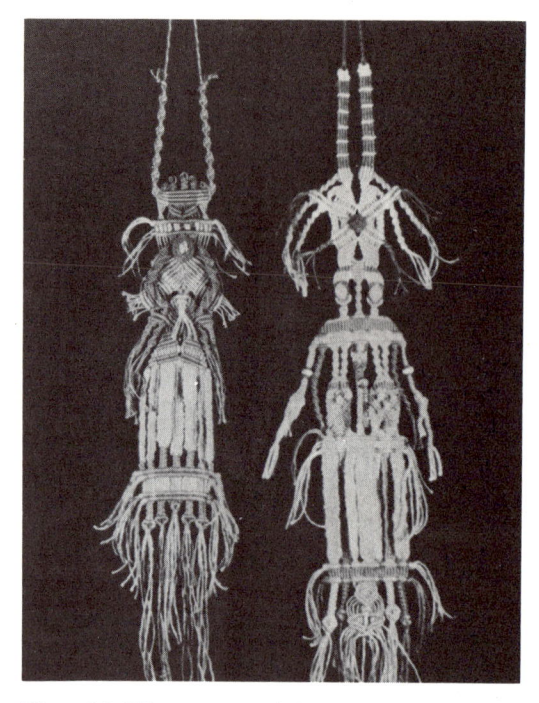

Illus. 84. Macramé and finger weaving were used to create these fanciful figures from cotton seine twine and synthetic rug yarns. If you are familiar with any non-loom methods of weaving, be creative in combining your skills with some macramé. Sprightly dolls such as these can add color and interest to any room.

TYPES OF WEAVING

A few examples of non-conventional looms are cardboard looms and frame looms. Driftwood is also a good base for weaving—the driftwood itself can become part of the total construction.

Cardboard Weaving

A cardboard loom is shown in Illus. 83. A piece of rigid cardboard about 10 inches × 12 inches is a good weaving area, but you can make your loom smaller or larger, as you need to. Cut notches along the top and bottom edges at the desired distances (usually determined by the thickness of the warp threads). When you intend to knot the warp ends after you have completed the weaving, pre-cut them long enough so that you have plenty of yarn to knot with. Mount the threads on the top notches and temporarily tie the ends at the bottom notches, releasing them as the tension increases or whenever necessary, as the weaving progresses. You can do the knotting right on the same cardboard, using T-pins to secure the work in place. Resume weaving after you have completed a small area of knots.

Illus. A 1. In this 22 inch × 30 inch wall hanging, macramé was combined with crocheting and wrapping. A variety of fibre materials—handspun wool, cotton, camel and goat hairs, and wool rug yarns—was used. White fox fur pieces were knotted into the piece.

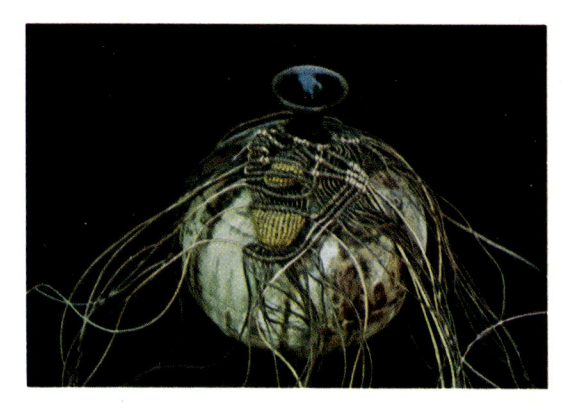

Illus. A 2. Macramé work in progress around a ceramic pot (by Lorraine Cillufo). Waxed and rough linen with polished India twine are being used.

Illus. A 3 (left). This 6½ inch × 14 inch neck piece was made with braided rayon cords in mostly Double Knots. An enamelled copper piece (by John Pesch) adorns the middle. The metallic piece on which the cords were mounted was a hand-mirror handle. The armatures are hollow cylindrical forms. Illus. A 4 (right). This 15 inch × 40 inch wall hanging combines macramé, crocheting and needle wrapping done with wool rug yarns and upholstery cord. The dowel was an old chair leg.

A

Illus. B 1. In this 6 inch × 8 inch weed pot, the macramé was done with jute cord. Wool rug yarn was used for the wrapping. A glass jar was used for shaping the pot and for support.

Illus. B 2 (above). Macramé, weaving and rug-hooking (Ghiordes Knots), using natural sisal fibres, polished India twine and wool rug yarns, resulted in this 15 inch × 45 inch wall hanging. (From the private collection of Elsie Winters.)

Illus. B 3 (left). Macramé, wrapping and rug-hooking, using primitive spun wool, synthetic yarns and jute cord were artfully combined in this 25 inch × 50 inch wall hanging. The enamelled piece in the middle is by John Pesch. Additional filler fibres were wrapped at the cord-ends to form a pile-like finish.

B

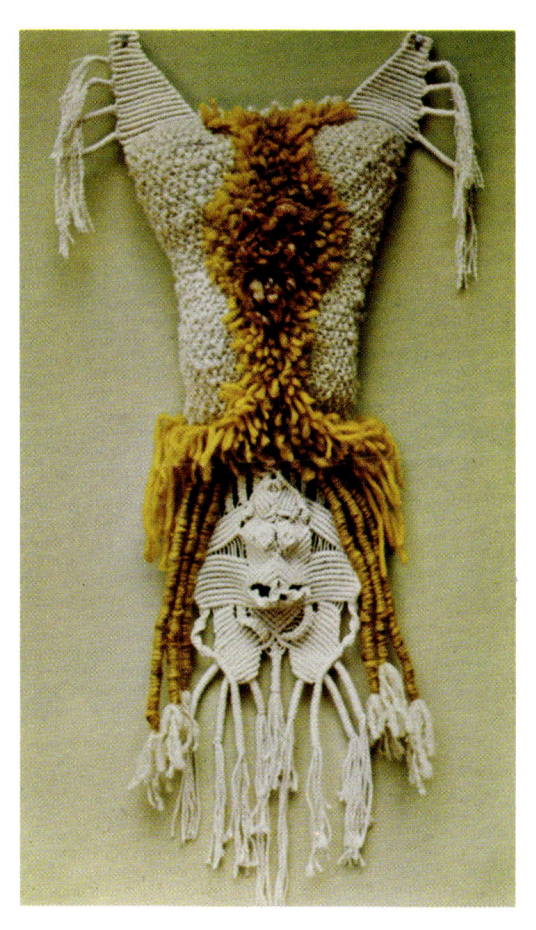

Illus. C 1 (above). Macramé, knitting, stuffing, wrapping and rug-hooking (Lark's Head Knots) were combined to create this 15 inch × 36 inch wall hanging, using light and heavy hand-spun wool yarns and cotton seine cords. Polyester fibre was used for stuffing.

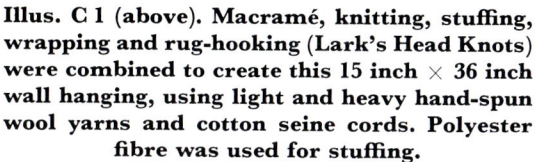

Illus. C 2 (top right). This 22 inch × 36 inch wall hanging consists of a piece of hand-woven fabric, used for hooking pile, which was then mounted on bamboo with a carved wood dowel. Long strands of primitive spun wool were wrapped next to macramé sennits. Cord-ends were left to form a rich pile at the bottom.

Illus. C 3 (bottom right). Macramé, weaving and rug-hooking (uncut pile) combined to create this 19 inch × 45 inch wall hanging. Wool rug yarns and primitive spun wool yarn were used. Aluminum wire formed the dowel. Dyed feathers were knotted at the cord ends.
The enamelled disc is by John Pesch.

Illus. D 1 (top left). Instructions for this 24 inch × 48 inch wall hanging begin on page 50. Macramé, weaving, rug-hooking and wrapping, with light and heavy wool rug, cotton and rayon novelty and synthetic yarns were used. Some weft threads were cut and then used for the macramé work as a means of joining the woven panels.

Illus. D 2 (above). Macramé, weaving and wrapping, done with heavy wool and synthetic yarns, wool fleece, camel and goat hairs were used to create this 20 inch × 45 inch wall hanging. The warp threads (synthetic yarns) were knotted around the middle shape and at the bottom in Flat Knots sennits. The cord-ends were wrapped with duck feathers.

Illus. D 3 (bottom left). Fur strips, as well as wool yarns and fleece, were used as weft material in this striking 16 inch × 21 inch wall hanging. Macramé and weaving, using heavy and regular wool rug yarns, wool fleece, and opossum fur strips, form the piece. Vertical Double Knots were worked out with warp threads between the woven areas.

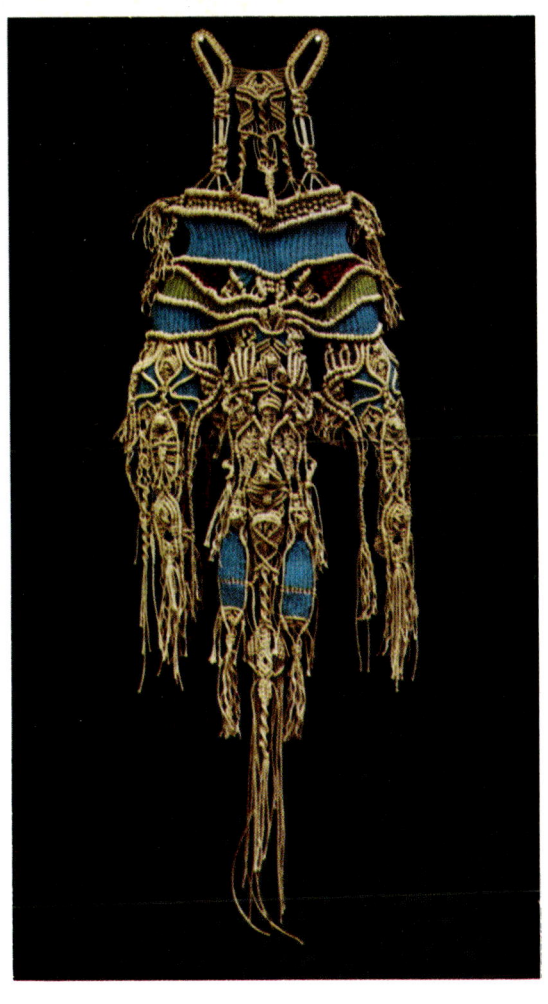

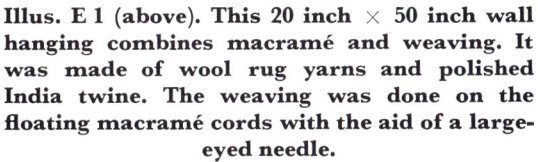

Illus. E 1 (above). This 20 inch × 50 inch wall hanging combines macramé and weaving. It was made of wool rug yarns and polished India twine. The weaving was done on the floating macramé cords with the aid of a large-eyed needle.

Illus. E 2 (top right). Entitled "Carnival Dancers," these three cylindrical figures suspended from a small hoop, measure 14 inches, 20 inches and 22 inches. Macramé, needle weaving and cardboard weaving, using mohair, colored sisal twines, rug yarn and mercerized cotton cords were used.

Illus. E 3 (bottom right). This stuffed tubular wall hanging with an enamelled piece (by John Pesch) embedded in the middle measures 12 inches × 25 inches. Polyester fibre was used for the stuffing.

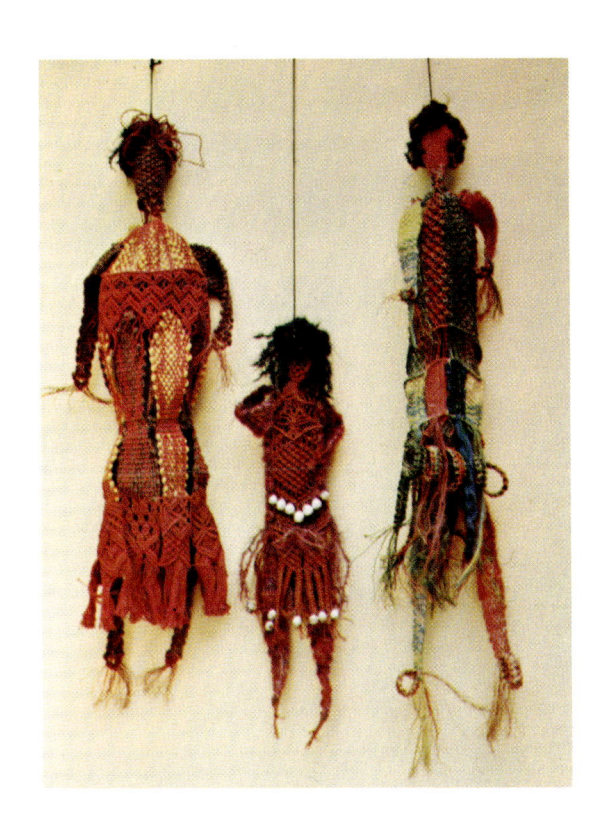

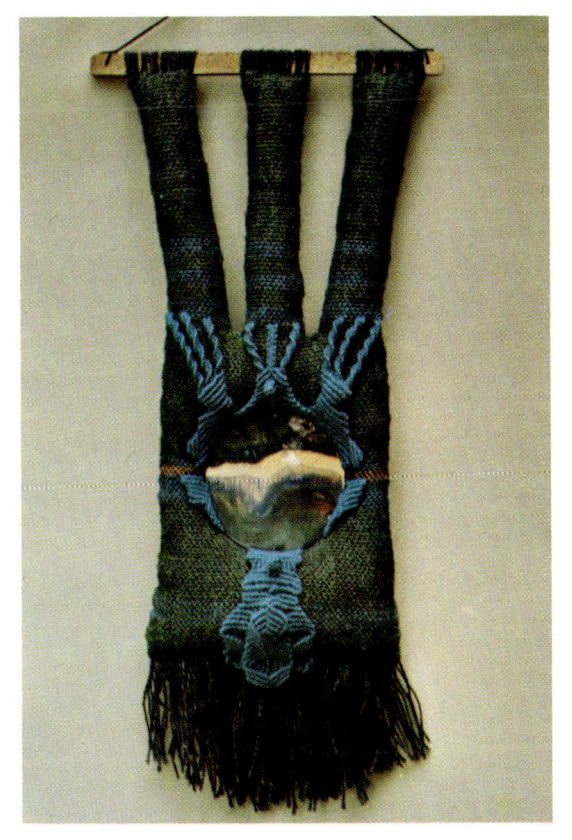

E

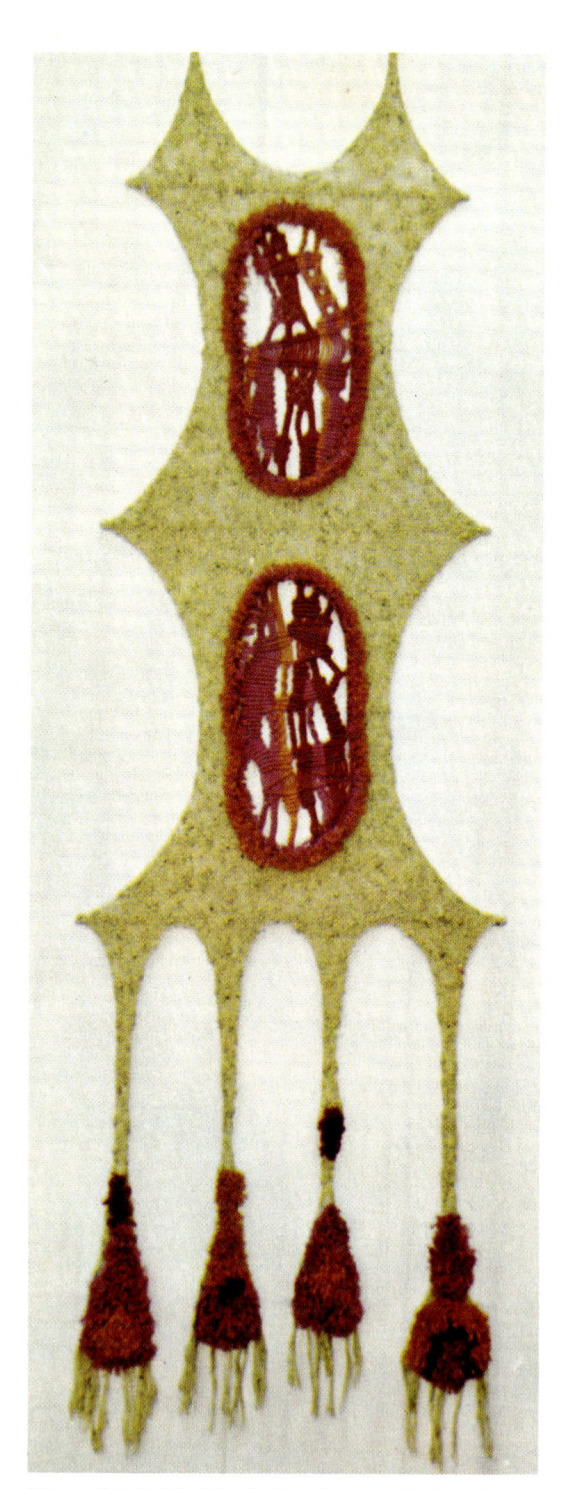

Illus. F 2. This 6 inch × 8 inch weed pot was shaped around a glass jar for support. Macramé, crocheting, needle wrapping and rug-hooking, using wool rug yarns and weaving yarns were used.

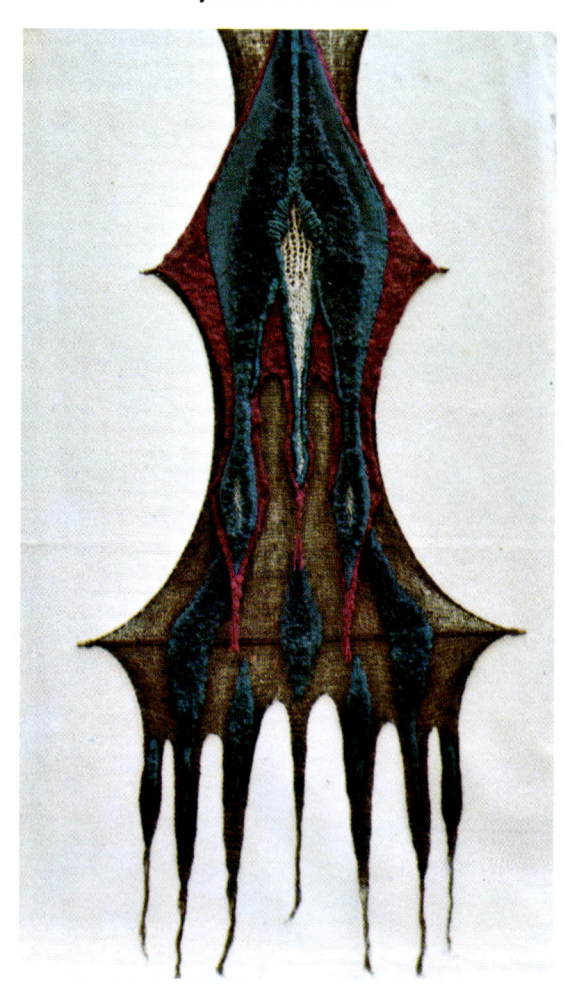

Illus. F 1 (left). The knitted part of this 25 inch × 100 inch wall hanging was created from troy-spun yarn (a blend of nylon, rayon, jute, and cotton). Avanti rug wool was used in the rug-hooking and macramé areas. Illus. F 3 (right). This two-layered knitted wall hanging, which measures 20 inches × 7 feet, also consists of a rug-hooking with an even pile and macramé. Rug yarns, weaving yarns and metallic thread, as well as primitive spun wool for the macramé work, were used. Wood stretchers emphasize the pointed forms.

Illus. G 1 (left). Macramé was worked into a mask-like structure at the middle of an unusual knitted construction to form this 18 inch × 94 inch wall hanging. The stockinette stitch alone was used to form all the shapes. Illus. G 2 (right). This wall hanging consists of stuffed velvet as a background for a web-like macramé construction with an enamelled piece (by John Pesch) embedded in the middle.

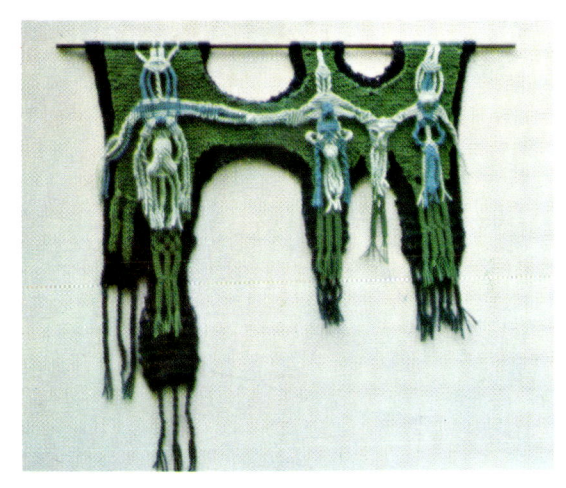

Illus. G 3 (left). This miniature wall hanging was constructed in such a way that it could be enlarged later. The macramé was worked over the two knitted layers. New strands of yarn, which were hooked onto the bottom edges of the knitted work, were later worked into macramé sennits. Illus. G 4 (right). A hand-woven 12 inch × 12 inch pillow was stuffed and used as the background for macramé work with hooked uncut pile.

G

Illus. H 1. Stuffed wool fabric forms the background for net-like macramé work (Flat Knots), with areas of hooked and wrapped yarns, in this 11 inch × 11 inch weed pot. A curved enamelled piece (by John Pesch) is embedded in the middle.

Illus. H 2 (right). This 24 inch × 38 inch wall hanging is entitled "King and His Jesters." It consists of macramé using natural jute and colored wool and cotton yarns decorated with ceramic beads (by Lorraine Cillufo) and shells.

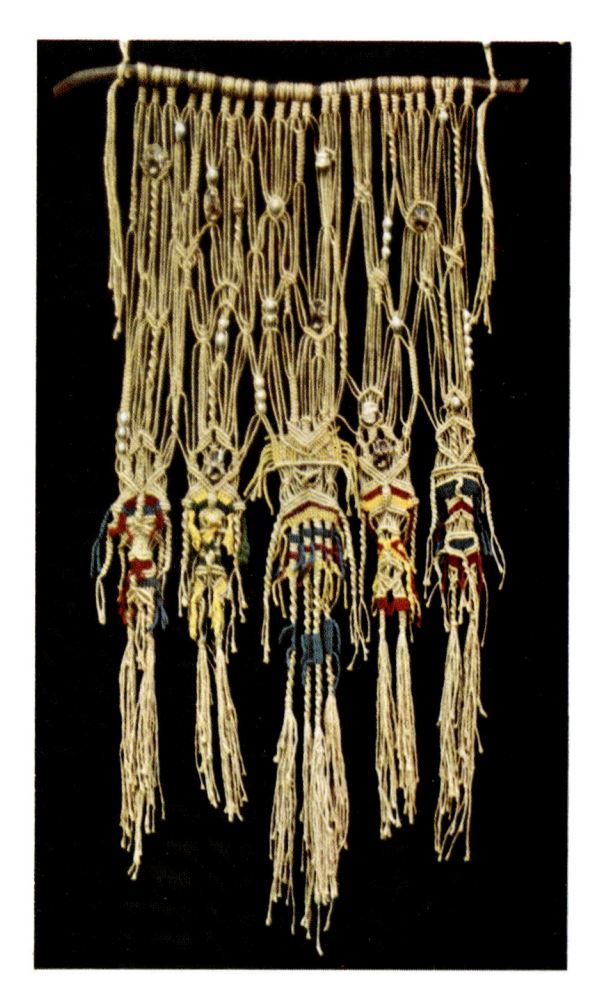

Illus. H 3 (left). This 6 inch × 8 inch macramé basket is made of synthetic rug yarn and cotton braided cord (as Knot Bearer). White fox fur strips were worked into the knotting. The cord-ends were wrapped as a finishing touch. Illus. H 4 (right). A gold bracelet was used for mounting braided rayon cords worked into Double Knots to form this 5 inch × 8 inch pendant. An opossum fur piece was knotted into the middle panel.

H

Illus. J 1. This striking neck piece measures 7 inches × 25 inches. Composed of macramé using marine cord with a punched leather piece as a starting point, it is enhanced by enamelled pieces (by John Pesch), feathers and hand-spun and dyed wool.

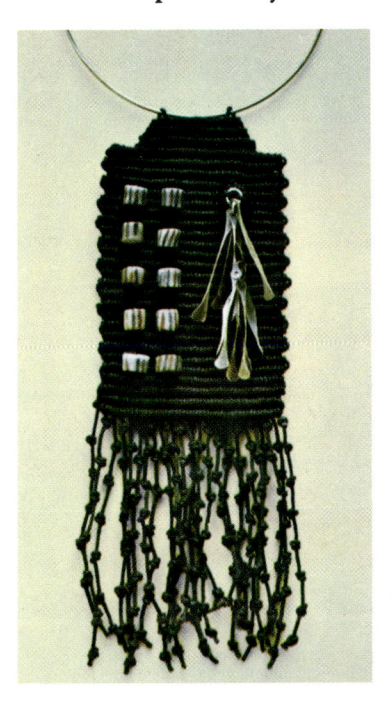

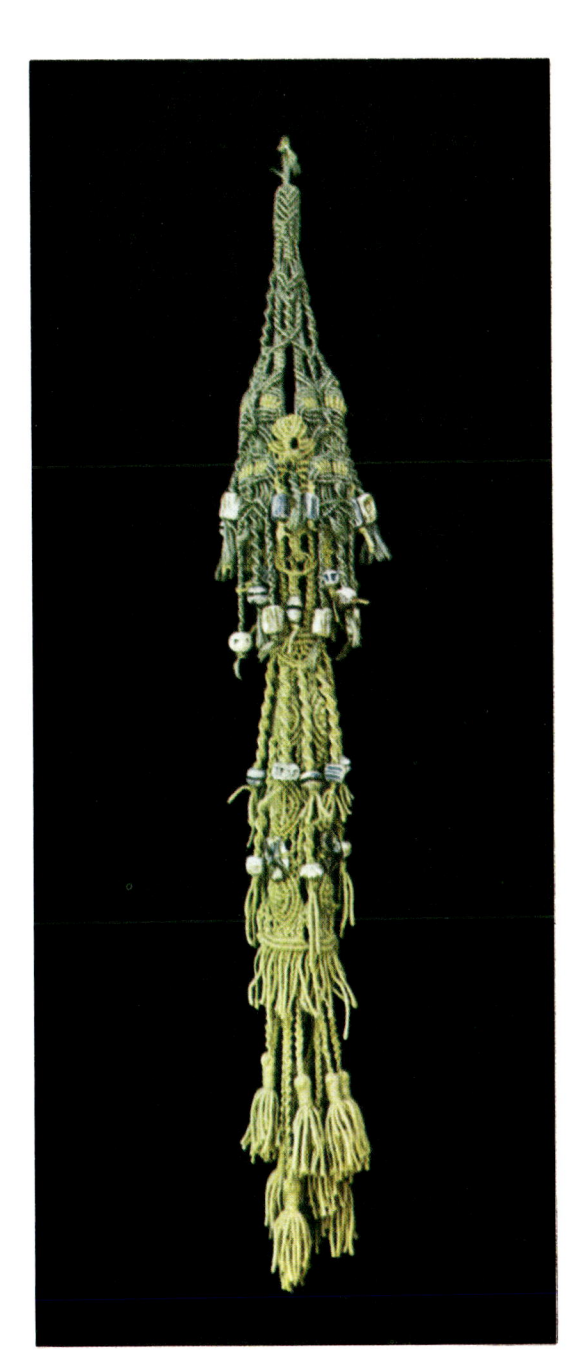

Illus. J 2. This 5 inch × 36 inch cylindrical hanging, made of rug wool and jute cord, is decorated with ceramic beads (by Lorraine Cillufo).

Illus. J 3. This 3½ inch × 7 inch neck piece was made of black marine cord, Indian trade beads and hammered silver forms (by Aniello Schettino). The rectangular shape was made up of Double Knots. Bead Knots were worked on each cord-end.

J

Illus. K 1. A macramé wig made of waxed linen and feathers adorns this 6½ inch × 23 inch whimsical ceramic chime (by Lorraine Cillufo).

Illus. K 2. Corn husks used as Knot Bearers and worked into Double Knots with synthetic rug yarn resulted in this 7 inch × 14 inch figure.

For round or circular weaving, use a circular cardboard loom instead of a rectangular one. The collar on the back cover was made on a circular cardboard loom.

Frame-Loom Weaving

A picture frame, like the one shown in Illus. 85, is a good base to use for frame-loom weaving. Hammer some nails right on the top of the frame at the desired distance apart. (You might prefer to use a separate block of wood on which you hammer nails and then screw it to the top of the frame. This facilitates your changing to the desired warping distances for different kinds of weaves.) For plain weave, the warping distances would be smaller than for tapestry weave.

Pre-cut the warp threads to lengths which allow enough extra for you to do the knotting work later, or after you have completed the weaving.

Tubular Weaving

For tubular weaving, you can use either a cardboard or a frame loom. Mount warp threads on both the front and back sides of the loom, and bring the weft around the sides to form a tubular weave. For an example of tubular weaving, see Illus. E3.

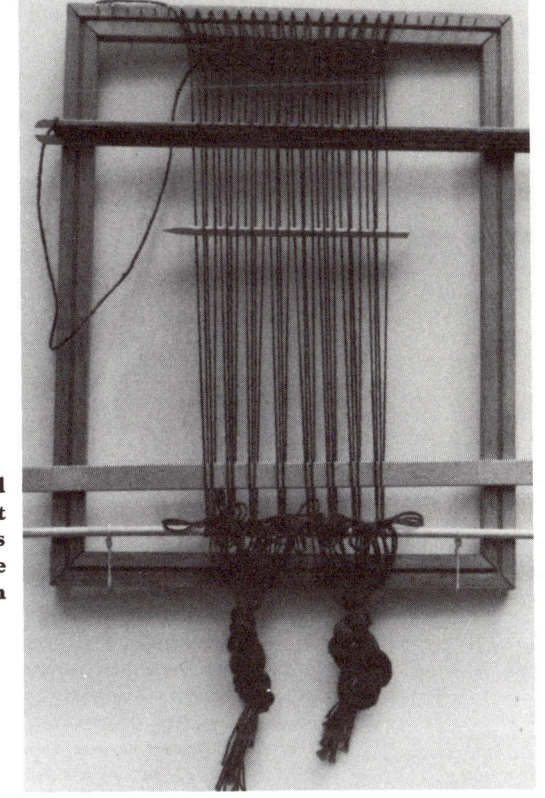

Illus. 85. Any spare picture frame you have is a good base for frame-loom weaving. Simply mount pre-cut lengths of yarn to use as warp threads from nails you hammer in at the top of the frame. Knot the extra lengths of yarn at the bottom to use later in your macramé.

WALL HANGING

Following are instructions for the colorful wall hanging in Illus. D1—an attractive combination of macramé, weaving, a little wrapping and rug-hooking. A tree branch was used as a dowel for mounting the three panels.

Materials
hand-spun and rug wool yarns
fleece
synthetic yarns
nubby cotton-rayon weaving yarns

Step 1: Weave on a long wood frame-loom, one panel at a time starting from the top, in tapestry weave (see Illus. 74). Each panel measures about 7 inches × 40 inches. See Illus. 86 for the weaving pattern. Then knot pile on between the rows of wefts for about 3 inches, using Ghiordes Knots (see Illus. 62). Use synthetic yarn, which is stronger than wool, as warping threads and hand-spun wool, rug yarn and cotton-rayon yarns together with some fleece as weft threads. Introduce new colors gradually in the weaving process.

Step 2: After weaving a length of 21 inches, use some cut rug yarns (a total of

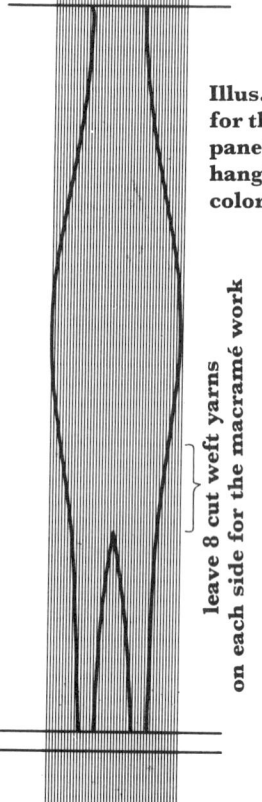

Illus. 86 (left). Pattern for the three woven panels in the wall hanging shown in color Illus. D1.

leave 8 cut weft yarns on each side for the macramé work

Illus. 87 (right). After you complete weaving the three panels of the hanging in Illus. D1, add some decorative macramé to join the panels together. Using eight cut weft threads on each side of each panel, follow the directions on page 51 to duplicate the macramé design shown here. You can, of course, improvise your own macramé segment, if you wish.

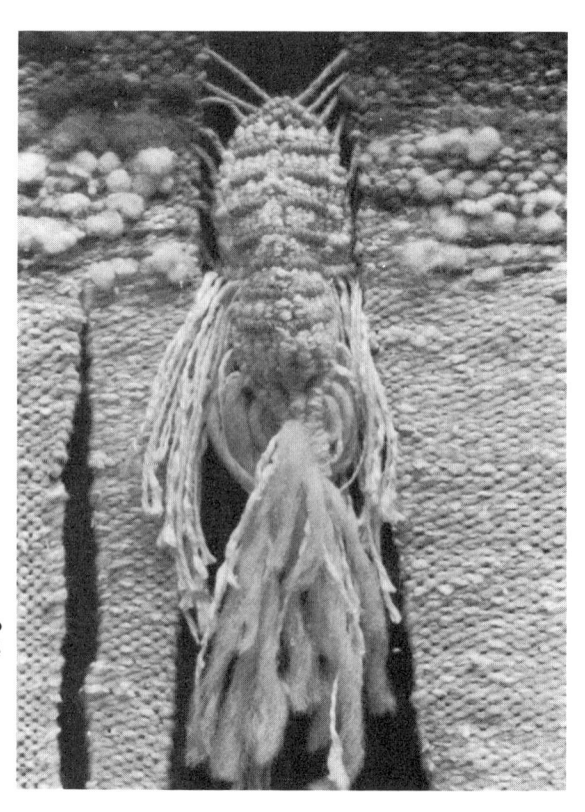

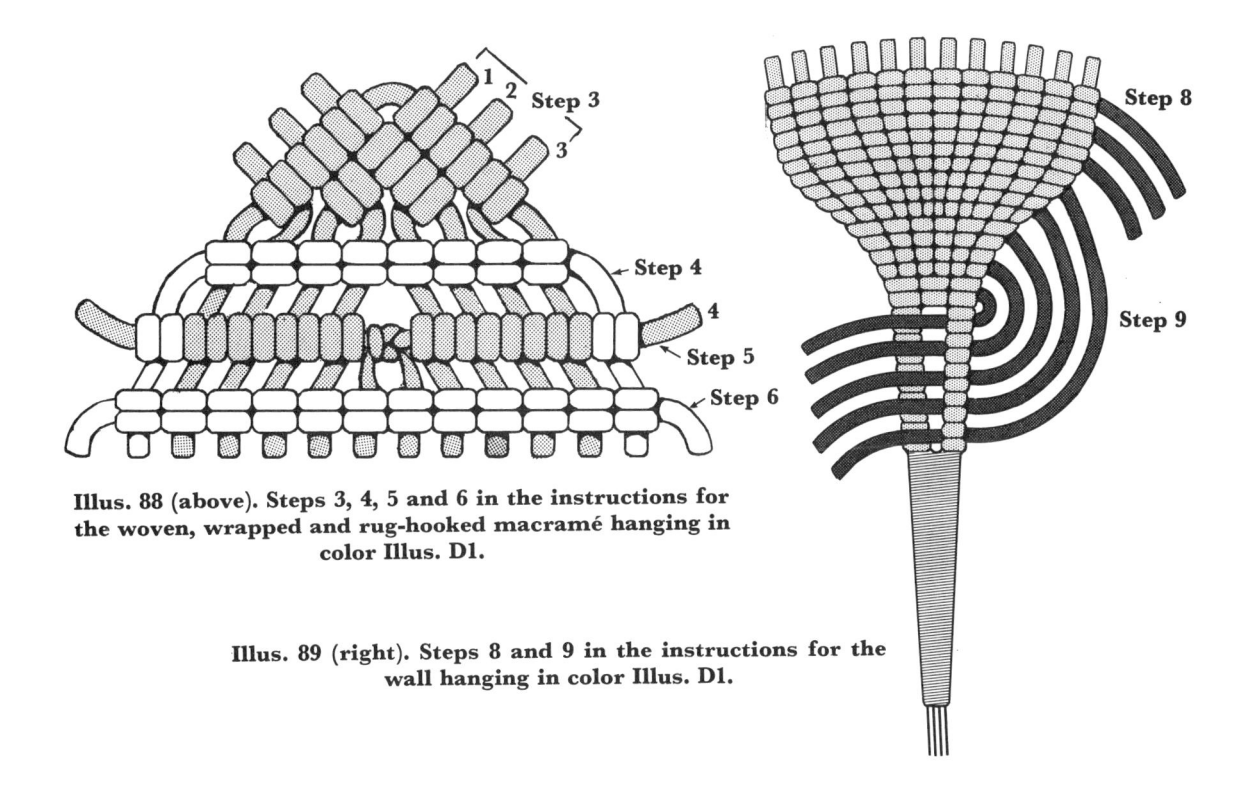

Illus. 88 (above). Steps 3, 4, 5 and 6 in the instructions for the woven, wrapped and rug-hooked macramé hanging in color Illus. D1.

Illus. 89 (right). Steps 8 and 9 in the instructions for the wall hanging in color Illus. D1.

8 strands on each side) as weft threads. These should be long enough to be used for macramé when you have completed the weaving.

Step 3: Then join these loose strands together using macramé. With the top 3 strands from each panel and using a new strand of rug yarn as KB, make 2 left and 2 right Diagonal DK Bars (about 1½ inches from each panel) between the panels.

Step 4: With a strand of a different color as WT, make Vertical DKs using all the other strands as KBs (see Illus. 88).

Step 5: With the next (fourth) strand from each panel as KBs, make a Horizontal DK Bar. Join these KBs at the middle into a SK (see Illus. 88).

Step 6: Repeat Steps 4 and 5 until you have made a total of 5 Horizontal DK Bars. (Use the same colors as before.)

Step 7: Pull the sixth strands from each side of the last Horizontal DK Bar together and knot into a SK (similar to Illus. 21) to raise the whole structure. Then repeat Steps 4 and 5 again (excluding the first 5 strands on both sides) two more times.

Step 8: Make Vertical DK Bars with 8 new Working Threads, but this time use 2 KB strands together in every row until only 3 Vertical DKs are left (see Illus. 89).

Step 9: Bringing back each of the 5 new strands WTs, and using them as WTs also, make one Vertical DK Bar on each side (using half of the middle KBs), letting all the ends hang out from the middle space (between the 2 Vertical DK Bars), as shown in Illus. 89. Wrap the remaining KB strands.

Step 10: Now use the remaining warp strands at the bottoms of the two outside woven panels. In groups of 4, and using new double strands (of nubby cotton-rayon yarns), make 4 spiral (Half Flat Knots) sennits. You can add more filler strands towards the ends to give a fuller pile-look.

Step 11: With the middle woven panel, you can wrap the remaining warp strands into three groups, adding filler strands as you wish towards the ends.

Step 12: Work 2 Vertical DK Bars at the outer sides using the remaining weft rug yarns (see Illus. 90). You can alternate additional strands of spun and nubby yarns with the rug yarns, as was done for the wall hanging in Illus. D1.

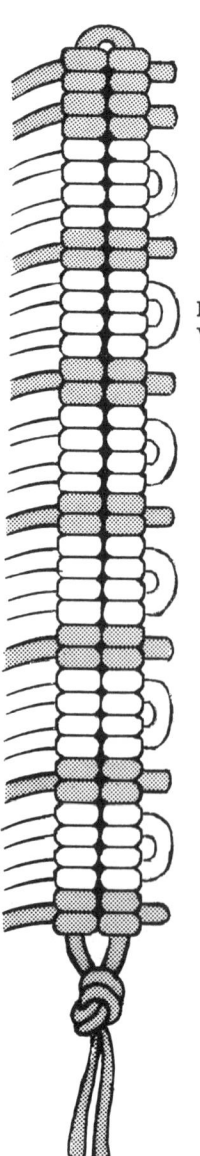

Illus. 90. Step 12 in the instructions for the hanging in color Illus. D1. Make two Vertical Double Knot Bars at the two outer edges to finish off the macramé addition to this creation.

Macramé Plus Crocheting

Like many textile craftspeople, you may know at least the basic crochet stitches. These are usually enough to enable you to create unique pieces involving crochet and macramé, by just using your imagination. Here again, remember that the technique of crochet is not nearly as important as the innovative forms or shapes that you can possibly construct. You are simply using crochet as a method of adding a new dimension to a macramé piece.

The basic crochet stitches, which are most useful in creating forms, are the chain stitch, single crochet, half double and double crochet stitches (UK: chain stitch, double crochet, half treble crochet and treble crochet). With the single crochet stitch alone (see Illus. 91), you can create sculptural shapes. You can make finger-like structures like those in Illus. 99 with half double crochet stitches, as shown in Illus. 92. You can make the strips short or long, as was shown in Illus. 93, where the strips were joined together while needle-wrapping cords in-between.

Illus. 91. You can use the single crochet stitch, shown here, to quickly create interesting sculptural shapes to use as a base for decorative macramé work.

Illus. 92. Finger-like appendages, which you can use to add special interest to your crochet sections, are easy to make using half double crochet stitches, as shown here.

Illus. 93. Crocheted strips joined together with needle-wrapped cores result in a strikingly textured pattern. Experiment in combining crocheting and other textile techniques with macramé.

As in weaving, you may work the crocheted areas either separately or simultaneously with macramé. In Illus. A1, the crochet pieces were knotted into the macramé work. At some points, they were stitched on. The appendages at the bottom corners were stitched on after the macramé was completed (see the close-up in Illus. 94). In Illus. 95, also a close-up of Illus. A1, note the mixture of different forms of crocheted structures with knotted and wrapped structures.

In Illus. 96, 97 and 98, the crocheted parts were first finished to fit over glass

Illus. 94. Contrasting yarn textures, as well as spiral and finger-like structures made with half double crochet stitches, formed this corner (the bottom left side) of the wall hanging in color Illus. A1. Remember that in creating fibre-art masterpieces, there are no "rules"—join together any techniques, colors and textures to form original, one-of-a-kind hangings.

Illus. 95. Notice how naturally crocheted tubes (from single crochet stitches), strips and spirals (using double crochet stitches), macramé Half Flat Knot sennits, Single Buttonhole Knot chains and wrapped cores group together. This artful collection of techniques forms the bottom right side of the wall hanging in color Illus. A1.

Illus. 96. A coffee jar was used for shaping and supporting this rustic weed pot which combines crochet and macramé. Wool rug yarns were used to do these techniques.

Illus. 97. This weed pot was also made from wool rug yarns using macramé and crochet. It was shaped around a wine bottle.

jars. Then, cords were hooked on and macramé was worked right on the jars, independently, until they were entirely covered.

Illus. 99 is another project in which all the crocheting was finished before the macramé (tentacle-like projections) was added by hooking on new cords at the top of the tubular forms.

INCREASE AND DECREASE

When you create sculptural forms using crochet, it is important to know how to increase and decrease the number of stitches. To increase the number of stitches, work two stitches in one stitch (of the preceding row). This forms one extra stitch. To decrease the number of stitches, work the first half of a stitch in one stitch (of the preceding row) and then another half stitch in the next stitch (of the preceding row). Draw the thread through all the loops on the hook, to finish the last stitch.

Illus. 98. This is a third example of how you can combine macramé and crochet, using wool rug yarns, to create a weed pot. As you can see, your own ingenuity determines how a weed pot you create, even using materials and techniques that are not unusual, can be totally unique. This weed pot was also shaped around a wine bottle. See what interestingly shaped containers you can find to use as supports for your work. (From the private collection of Aurora Fe Moya.)

Illus. 99. Creative use of macramé sennits added to a crocheted area resulted in this unique sculpture. Regular and heavy rug yarns and mohair were combined artistically to construct the piece.

MACRAMÉ AND CROCHET SCULPTURE

Here are instructions for the unusual sculptured piece in Illus. 100, which creatively combines macramé, crocheting, hooking and a little wrapping.

Materials
rug yarn and mohair (for the crocheted areas)
nubby cotton-rayon weaving yarn
horse hair

Illus. 100. This is one view of the sculptured creation whose directions begin on the next page. The upper half of the free-form sculpture was crocheted, while the lower half was made from Horizontal Double Knot Bars. Rug-hooking was used to knot on the yarn for the macramé, as well as accent strands of horse hair.

Illus. 101. In this view of the sculpture in Illus. 100, you can see the random placement of rug yarns wrapped with nubby yarn that add to the total effect of this creation. The cylindrical single crocheted projections attached to the top were finished off with a row of mohair for contrast.

Step 1: Start by crocheting a cylindrical form, using rug yarn, in single crochet, 4 inches in diameter and about 4 inches high.

Step 2: Then crochet the 10 tubular projections at the top (in single crochet) separately, using the same rug yarn and ending each with a row of mohair yarn.

Step 3: Stitch the finished tubular structures together at their bases onto the 4-inch cylindrical body (see Illus. 102).

Step 4: Hook on new strands of rug yarn and nubby cotton-rayon weaving yarn

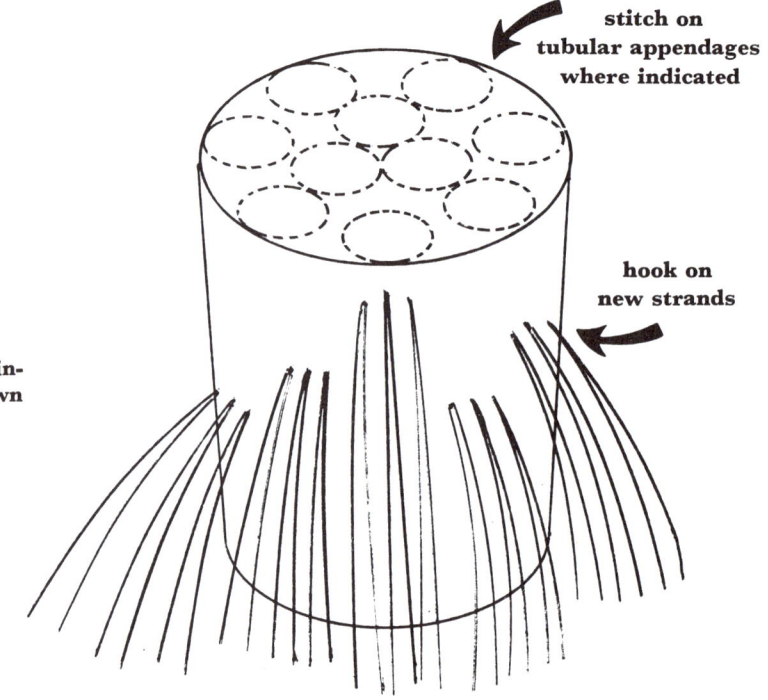

Illus. 102. Steps 3 and 4 in the instructions for the sculpture shown in Illus. 100 and 101.

stitch on tubular appendages where indicated

hook on new strands

58

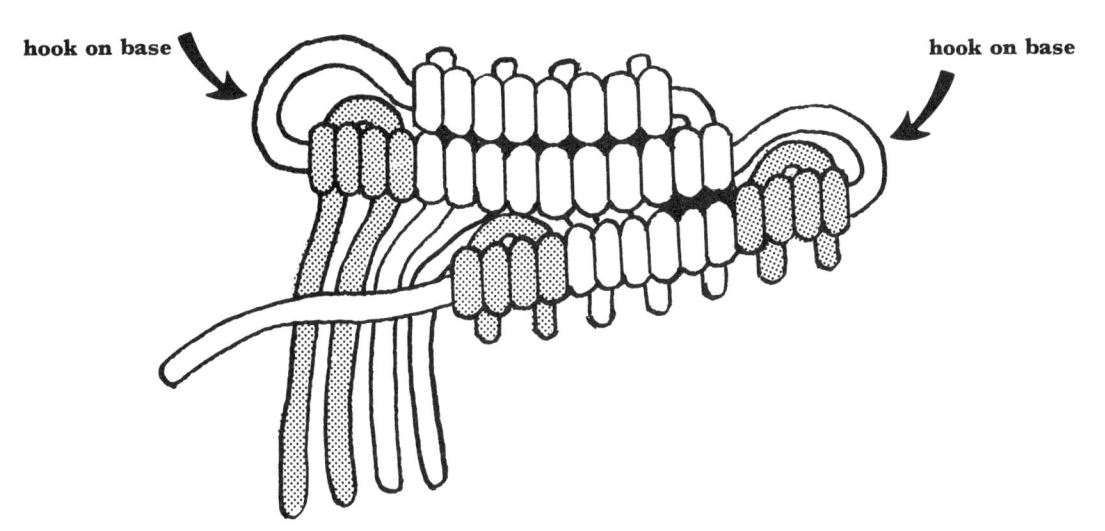

Illus. 103. Step 4 in the instructions for the sculpture in Illus. 100 and 101. Increase the number of Working Threads as shown.

at different points along the sides of the body (see Illus. 102). Then knot downwards in Horizontal DK Bars, using rug yarn as KBs. Increase the number of WTs gradually by adding more new strands whenever necessary to form the raised structures (see Illus. 103). (See also Illus. 17 for making Horizontal DK Bars using a single cord as KB.) Tuck all the cord-ends in. Knot horse hair on at different points on the body.

Step 5: Now, trace the outline of the base on paper and then work this shape out in single crochet. Stitch this piece to the bottom of the macramé to form a flat bottom.

Step 6: You can stitch on some strands of rug yarn, vertically, against the sides of some of the tubular projections and then wrap them with the nubby yarn, using a yarn needle. You can also hook on rug yarn at the bases of the tubular projections, using the cut-pile method shown in Illus. 63.

Macramé Plus Knitting

When you combine macramé with knitting, you will find that the macramé looks better used as an accent rather than as an equally important technique. In Illus. F1, for instance, new threads were hooked on the border of the oval area, and the knots were worked out independently of the knitting. A close-up is shown in Illus. 104. In Illus. 105, the macramé was also worked out separately over the knitted surface as an additional decoration and textural contrast.

Illus. 104. This close-up shows the macramé portion of the knitted wall hanging in color Illus. F1. The simplicity of the knitted area makes the macramé knotting especially outstanding.

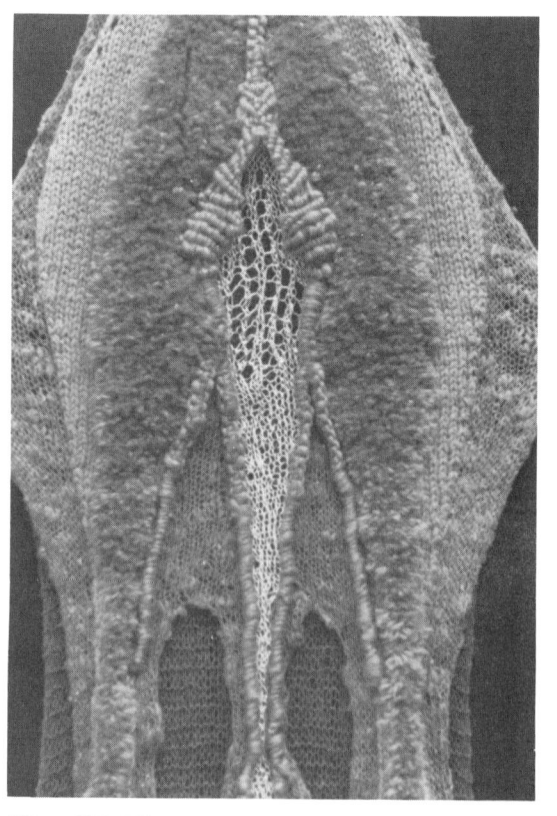

Illus. 105. The two-layered knitted background in this close-up of color Illus. F3 is subtly emphasized by even-piled rug-hooking and macramé.

Illus. 106. The stockinette stitch (all knit in one row, and all purl in the next) is one of the most basic knitting stitches. As you can see in the top portion of this photograph, the simplicity of the stitch makes it quite suitable to use as a background for intricate macramé work. You can easily hook cut cords to the bottom of the knitted area to use for your macramé, as you can see in the bottom part of this photograph.

The choice of materials in knitting is always an important consideration, as it directly affects the surface texture. For this reason, you might prefer to use rug yarns or weaving yarns instead of the commercial knitting yarns for wall hangings.

In the pieces shown in this book, the knitted forms are more important in the construction than the technique of knitting itself. You can easily use the simplest and most basic knitting stitches and still achieve impressive effects. In Illus. G1, for example, a plain stockinette stitch was used, all knit stitch on one side and all purl stitch on the other. (Illus. 106 shows the stockinette stitch.) Note that the sides or edges tend to curl back with the stockinette stitch, as with the tubular appendages in the same piece.

In Illus. F1 and C1, the moss stitch was used (knit one, purl one, and so on, on one side and the reverse on the other side) (see Illus. 107). In Illus. 108 and G3, the

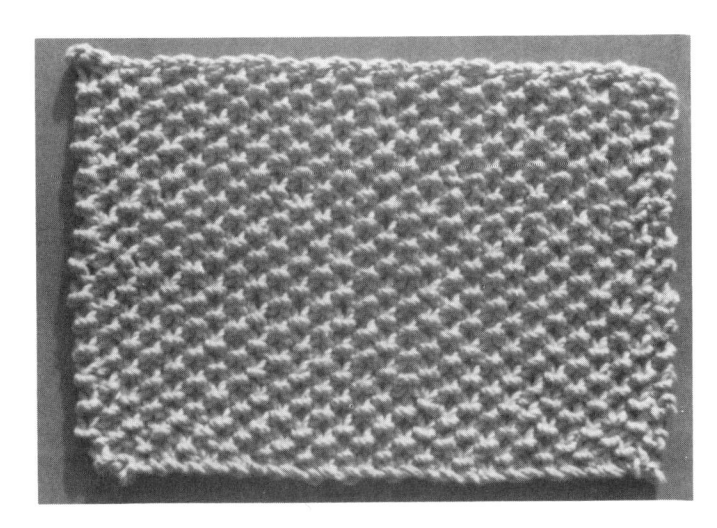

Illus. 107. The moss stitch, pictured here, is another basic knitting stitch you can use to form the background for creative macramé work. The moss stitch consists of knitting one stitch, then purling one stitch, and so on across one row, doing the reverse on the next row.

Illus. 108. This sample shows plain knitting, which consists of all knit stitches on both sides.

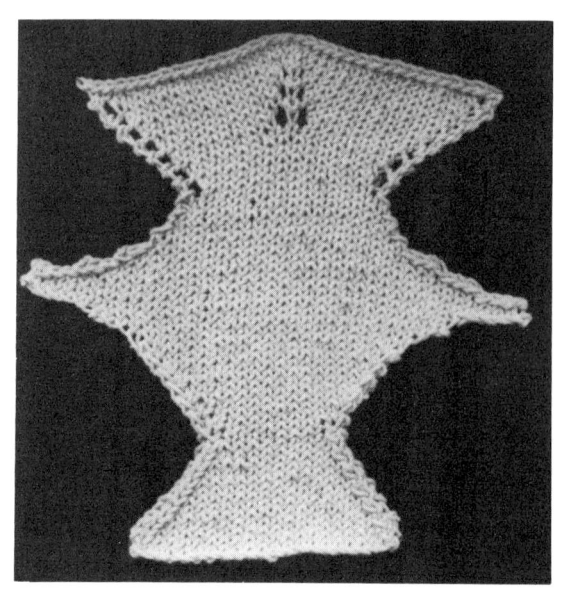

Illus. 109. By increasing or decreasing the number of knitted stitches, you can create unusual shapes to work with.

knit stitch was used on both sides. These two last patterns do not cause the sides to curl up, as the stockinette does, and thus, a more or less flat piece is the result.

To create different shapes, you increase or decrease the stitches along the sides. Illus. 109 shows various shapes you can create if you either add on or drop out stitches. In Illus. F1 and F3, wood stretchers were used to emphasize the pointed forms.

You can use either of two methods to decrease stitches in knitting: knit two together; or slip one, knit one, slip stitch over. Two methods you can use to increase stitches are: knit one without slipping the stitch from the preceding row off the needle and then continue knitting the new row; or yarn over, then continue to knit the row.

As always, it is only through experimenting and exploring your materials that you will find innovative ways to combine macramé and knitting.

HAND-KNITTED HANGING

The unique hand-knitted wall hanging in Illus. G1 (whose instructions follow) was done entirely in the stockinette stitch (see Illus. 106), but you can certainly use any knit stitches you want for your creation.

Materials
spun wool yarn (for the knitted areas)
synthetic yarns

fleece
feathers
jute cord (for the macramé area)

You make the knitted portion of the hanging in Illus. G1 in two parts, which you join together after you have knitted them.

Step 1: Start with two separate balls of yarn and cast on 10 stitches with each. Form the shapes by increasing and decreasing the number of stitches along the sides, as you wish (see Illus. 109).

Step 2: When both knit sections are the length you want, you knit the tentacle-like structures at both sides. Work with 5 stitches at a time, also in the stockinette stitch, to a length of about 77 to 80 inches. (You can slip the remaining stitches onto a stitch holder as you work on the different tentacles.)

Step 3: Then mount the body, which measures 15 inches × 18 inches wide, by sewing along the sides, onto a stuffed fabric of the same shape and size. Knit the middle grape-like structures separately, stuff and then stitch them together to form a bunch. You can hook additional pile onto the underside, using synthetic yarns.

Step 4: Now start the macramé area at the middle by hooking on four loops of jute cord. Illus. 110 shows a close-up of the macramé work.

Illus. 110. This is a close-up of the macramé area in the middle of the knitted wall hanging shown in color Illus. G1. Wool fleece and feathers add interest to the mask-like macramé construction.

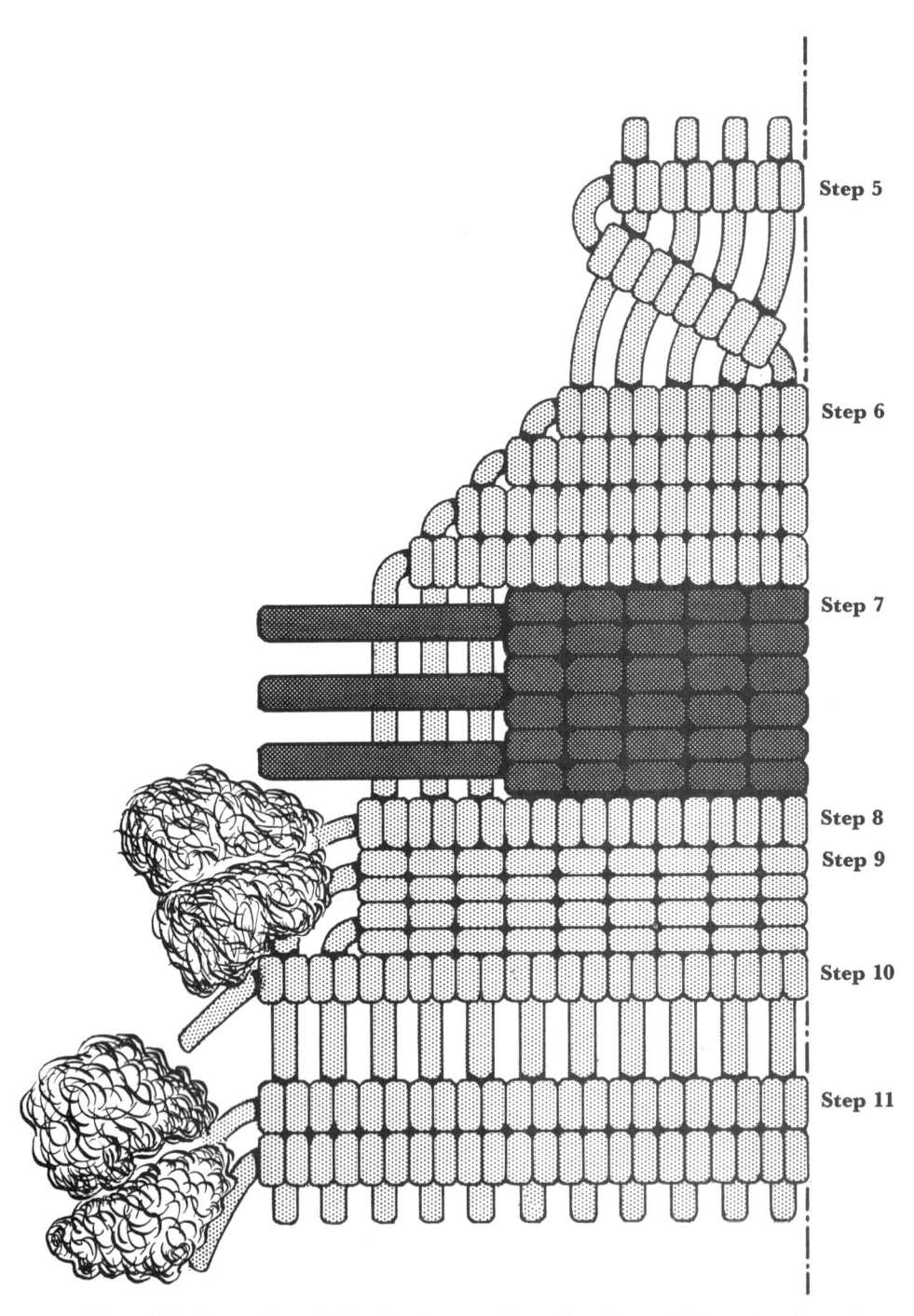

Illus. 111. Steps 5 to 11 in the instructions for the wall hanging in color Illus. G1. Note that this only shows the left half of the macramé section.

64

Step 5: Make one Horizontal DK Bar, then a right and left Diagonal DK Bar (see Illus. 111).

Step 6: Add new KB cords for every row of 4 successive Horizontal DK Bars (see Illus. 21 and 111).

Step 7: Introducing 3 strands of spun yarn (dark purple was used), make 3 rows of 10 Vertical DKs (see Illus. 26, left, and Illus. 111).

Step 8: Make another Horizontal DK Bar, using a new KB jute cord. Knot fleece on at both ends of the bar (see Illus. 111).

Step 9: Using 2 strands of synthetic yarn, make 2 rows of Vertical DKs (see Illus. 111).

Step 10: Make another Horizontal DK Bar using a new KB jute cord (see Illus. 111).

Step 11: Allow a space of ½ inch before making 2 more Horizontal DK Bars (using a new KB each row). Again, knot fleece at both ends of the first bar (see Illus. 111).

Step 12: Using 4 strands of spun yarn, make 4 rows of 22 Vertical DKs, similar to the Vertical DKs you added in Step 7.

Step 13: Make another Horizontal DK Bar, using a new KB jute cord.

Step 14: At the middle, make 10 Vertical DK Bars, using 4 new strands of synthetic yarn. Then finish off with a Horizontal DK Bar (using a new KB), knotting some black feathers into both sides of this bar. Pull the ends of the KB together and knot (SK) at the underside in order to create a tubular effect (see Illus. 112).

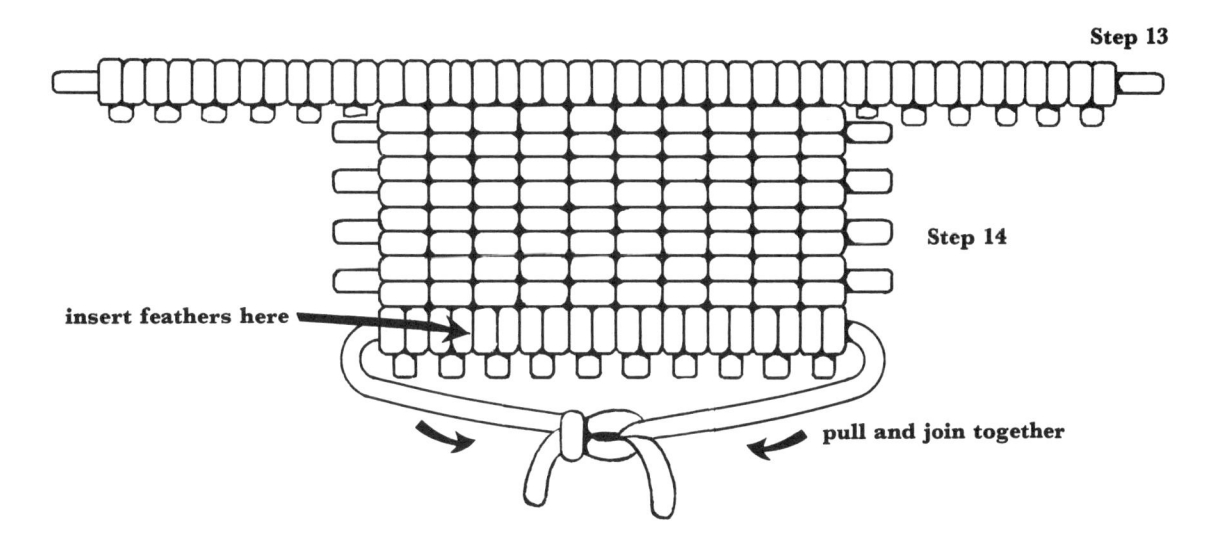

Illus. 112. Steps 13 and 14 in the instructions for the wall hanging in color Illus. G1.

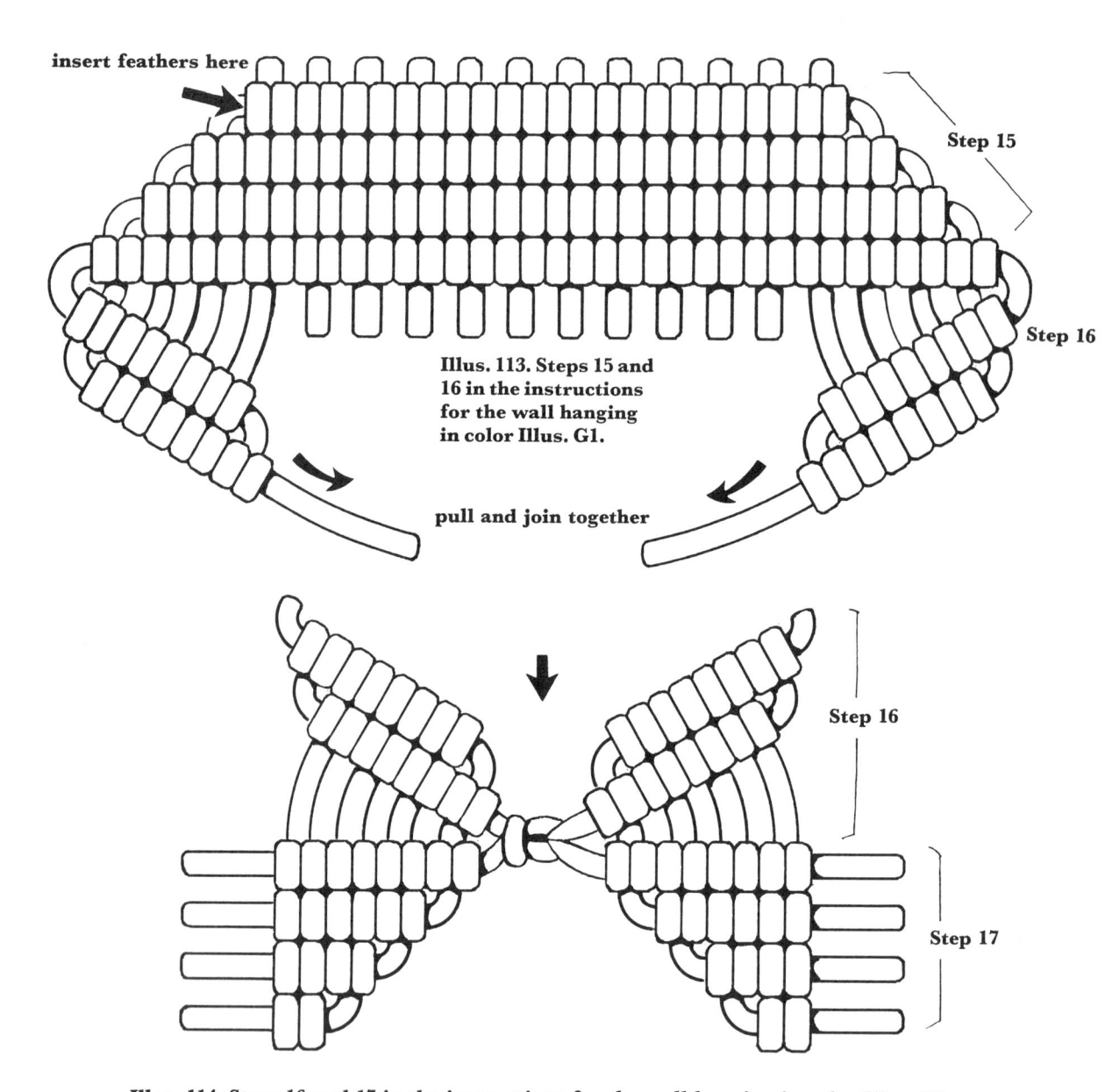

Illus. 113. Steps 15 and 16 in the instructions for the wall hanging in color Illus. G1.

insert feathers here

Step 15

Step 16

pull and join together

Step 16

Step 17

Illus. 114. Steps 16 and 17 in the instructions for the wall hanging in color Illus. G1.

Step 15: Make 4 more Horizontal DK Bars (omitting the middle projection) beneath, knotting more feathers into both sides of the first bar.

Step 16: With each 5 cords (on each side), make 2 right and left closed Diagonal DK Bars (see Illus. 113) separately, and then pull and join them together at the middle (under all 10 middle cords) with a SK (see Illus. 114).

Step 17: Then bring the inside cords towards the sides, by using each as KBs to make 4 close-open multiple Horizontal DK Bars. Trim the cord-ends to the desired lengths.

Macramé Plus Stuffing

Fabric stuffing results in soft sculptural forms of any shape you choose and good bases for your macramé work. Pillows are, of course, ideal stuffed surfaces for macramé work, but you can achieve striking effects with other stuffed forms as well. No matter what stuffed shape you choose, where and how you add the decorative macramé is an artistic decision. In the wall hanging in Illus. C1, as well as the pillow in Illus. G4, for example, cords were anchored right onto the edge of the stuffed fabric. You can also decorate a stuffed fabric with hooked pile, which was done in Illus. C1 and 115. You might even plan to leave some stuffed areas without macramé, if the

Illus. 115. A piece of commercially woven fabric was stuffed with polyester fibre to produce this unique wall hanging. Primitive spun yarn and rug yarns were used to do the macramé, wrapping and rug-hooking which add color and texture to this outstanding creation. The stuffing technique allows a special freedom in deciding the shape you wish to make your creation.

surface is interesting enough. In Illus. G2, G4 and H1, for instance, the macramé cords were worked into lacey, net-like structures so that the weaving or fabric shows through.

A stuffed printed or batiked surface also makes an exciting background for macramé work, especially if you tie in the designs and color schemes. Also, you can ornament a stuffed form with a colorful art object like an enamel piece, as in the tubular stuffed weaving in Illus. E3. The color of the enamel was picked up in the weaving and macramé yarns. Cords were also hooked onto the woven surface of the stuffing. The neatly finished macramé resulted in a pronounced color contrast which adds to the overall effect.

STUFFED WALL HANGING

The stuffed wall hanging shown in Illus. G2 was constructed by using a stuffed pillow (with an irregular shape) which served as a base for the macramé work. Black velvet fabric was chosen to contrast with the macramé work. Instructions follow for this unusually shaped creation.

Materials
rough linen cord (double strands)
enamelled disc or other decoration to imbed in the middle

Step 1: First trace the outline of the enamelled disc (or whatever decorative object you plan to use) on the pillow cover. Then sew round the traced area to create a depression.

Step 2: Fill the pillow with polyester fibre and glue the disc in place in the recessed area.

Step 3: Start macramé around this disc, with a DK Bar, using a separate strand as the KB.

Step 4: Work successive DK Bars on at different distances in a counter-clockwise direction, inserting a few knots, such as FK sennits, Vertical DK Bars or Bead Knots here and there between rows of DK Bars, until you have covered about three quarters of the lower area with the macramé work (see Illus. 116).

Step 5: Work a network of different sennits at the top area (see Illus. 10 and 31).

Step 6: With the aid of a needle, tuck in cord-ends at the top area into the pillow and through the back side. Secure.

Step 7: Leave the cord-ends at the bottom hanging down and cut them to the desired lengths. You can knot on additional cut strands, using Lark's Head Knots, to form the pile at the lower middle area.

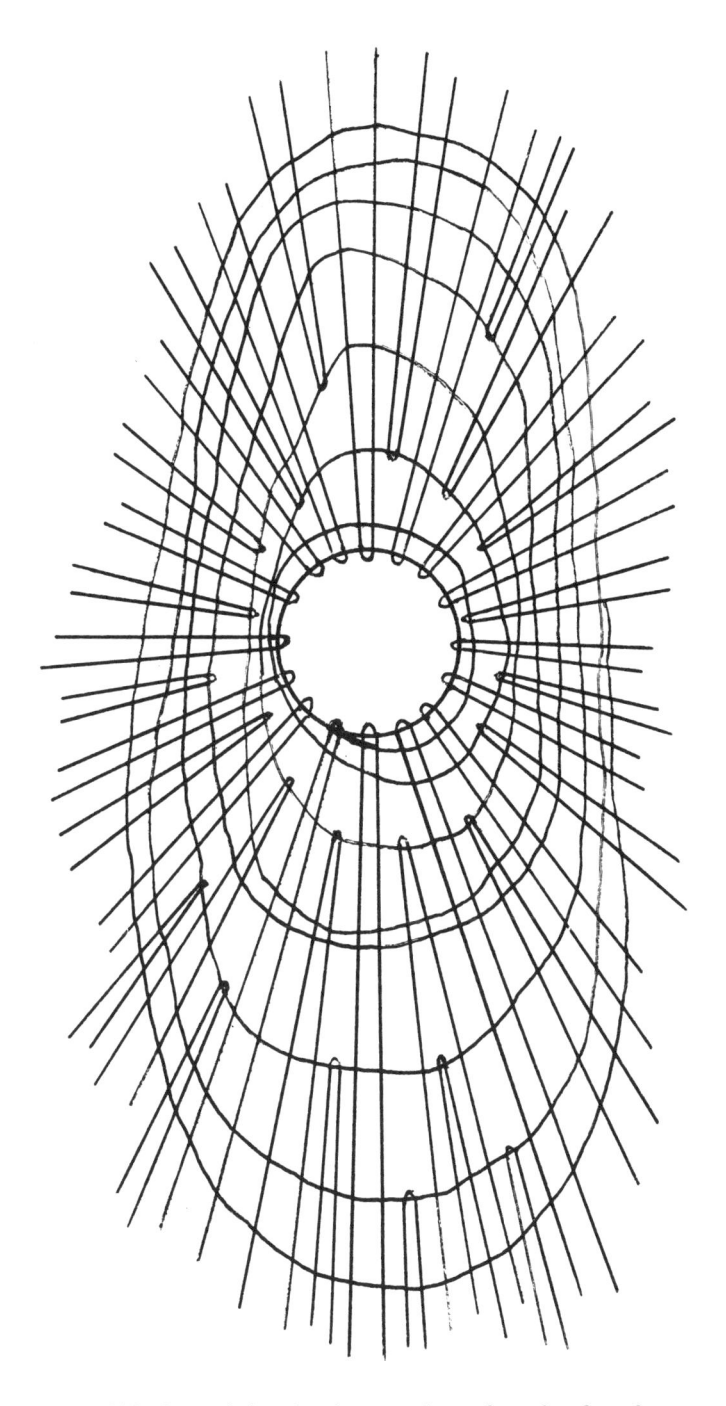

Illus. 116. Step 4 in the instructions for the free-form stuffed sculpture in color Illus. G2. You work circular Double Knot Bars in a counter-clockwise direction, adding on new Working Threads whenever necessary.

Macramé Plus Anything

You can creatively and effectively incorporate many objects, either natural or man-made, into macramé pieces. Use these objects to impart a new dimension, color or texture, to enhance your design as an integral part of it or to supplement the whole construction.

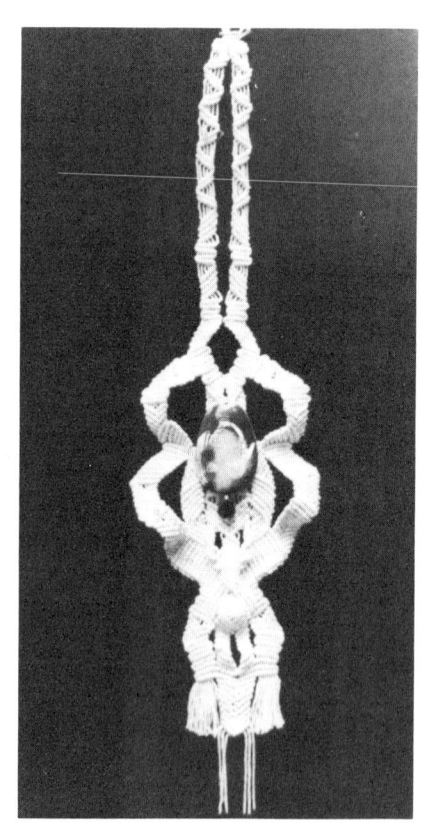

Illus. 117. White cotton, black glass beads and a black-and-white enamelled disc (by John Pesch) comprise this macramé neck piece. The lower part (Double Knot Bars) is shown close-up in Illus. 25.

Illus. 118. Ceramic beads tied to the macramé cord-ends combine artistically and naturally with macramé, as you can see in this close-up of color Illus. J2.

Illus. 119 (left). Do you need a hanger for a plant? Try making one from macramé. Here, a hand-formed ceramic pot (by Dorothy Pesch) is suspended from and decorated with macramé using marine cord and bamboo and wooden beads. Flat Knots and sennits make up the cylindrical form directly beneath the pot.

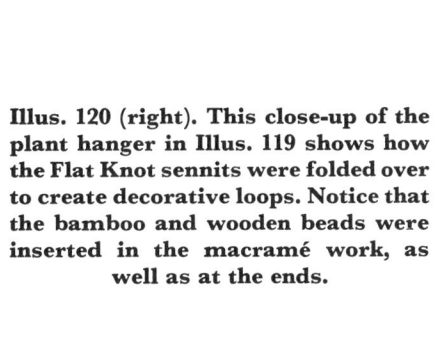

Illus. 120 (right). This close-up of the plant hanger in Illus. 119 shows how the Flat Knot sennits were folded over to create decorative loops. Notice that the bamboo and wooden beads were inserted in the macramé work, as well as at the ends.

You may knot whatever objects you choose into the piece during the macramé process or add pieces on later by either tying or glueing them at points where they show to best advantage. Take care, in choosing materials, to consider their size, shape, color and textural qualities in relation to the fibre materials you plan to use in the same piece. Decorative objects may either complement or contrast with macramé, but you do not want the two to clash. Experience and imagination will help you create skillful combinations.

Some materials are more frequently combined with macramé than others. Beads are successfully and commonly used in a wide range of sizes, shapes, colors and textures as decorative accents. In Illus. 120, for example, wood and bamboo beads were inserted in the knotting and at the cord-ends; in Illus. 118, ceramic beads add interest to the whole construction.

Many natural objects offer great diversity in texture or shape for your macramé projects. Plant matter (dried twigs, leaves and flowers, tree barks, driftwood and seeds), bones, rocks and shells, feathers, leather and fur strips—all of these have vast possibilities for you to work with. Illus. 119 and 121 show examples of how some of these objects have been used. See the color section for additional examples.

Illus. 121. This close-up of the macramé work attached to the large ceramic pot on the front cover is a good example of combining ceramic beads and duck feathers with macramé.

Ceramic pieces, some of them expressly designed for combining with macramé, make excellent starting points for macramé pieces or hangings. Refer to Illus. 122 and the color section for examples of this.

Other man-made materials, such as copper enamels, bells, jewelry pieces (see Illus. 123 and J3), glass, hardware, carved wood, and so on, have been beautifully incorporated into macramé work.

Junk shops and rummage sales offer good hunting grounds for unusual objects. From these places, you can accumulate a huge collection of intriguing pieces from old chair legs or backs, to jewelry, furs and hat feathers to inspire your creation.

Illus. 122. This is the back of the ceramic chime with a macramé "wig" shown in color Illus. K1. Simply shaped items can be just as attractive as intricate ones, especially if you combine several techniques and materials in a single creation.

Illus. 123. A silver clip was incorporated into this simply shaped neck piece. An opossum fur strip knotted into the last two Double Knot Bars adds a spark of individuality to this elegant neck piece.

Sometimes, you might even like to select a special article of personal interest or value to give your combined art piece a very subjective or even nostalgic quality.

MACRAMÉ, BEAD AND SILVER NECK PIECE

The neck piece in Illus. J3 is a beautiful example of beads and silver incorporated with macramé.

Materials
black marine cotton cord
silver neck ring
hammered silver rods
Indian trade beads

Step 1: Start the work for this neck piece with a DK Bar with 6 picots or loops (12 strands) (see Illus. 19).

Step 2: Make 2 more successive DK Bars, using a new KB each time, thus increasing the total number of strands (Illus. 21 shows how to introduce new KBs successively).

Step 3: Using a very long new strand as KB, add 2 new picots on each side, making a total of 26 DKs on the fourth DK Bar. From this point on, bring the same

73

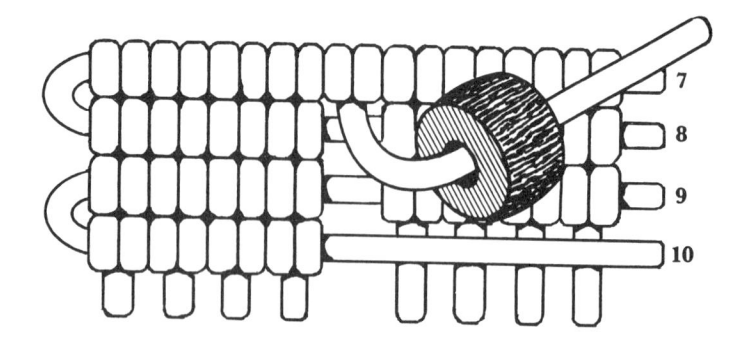

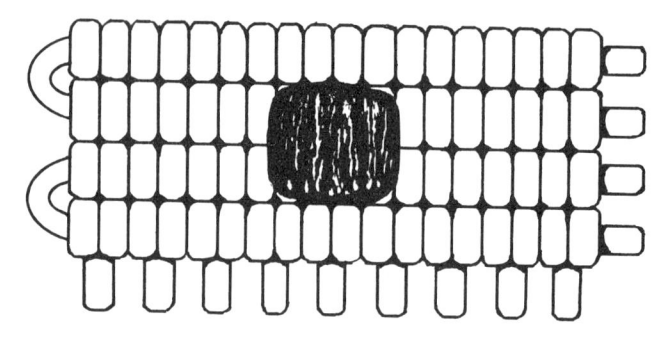

Illus. 124. This illustration of Step 6 in the instructions for the neck piece shown in color Illus. J3 shows how to insert a bead in the eighth Double Knot Bar.

KB left and right to form the rest of the DK Bars (see Illus. 17 for making Horizontal DK Bars using a single cord as KB).

Step 4: Make 2 more DK Bars.

Step 5: On strand #20 of the seventh DK Bar, construct a rose bud using 6 strands. (See page 33 for how to make a rose bud.) Tie a bunch of hammered silver rods at the middle of the bud, if you wish.

Step 6: Simultaneously, insert an Indian trade bead on strands #5 and #10 (of the eighth DK Bar). (Pick up the strands again on the tenth DK Bar, as shown in Illus. 124.) Repeat this process every 5 rows, to make a total of 10 beads.

Step 7: Make as many more rows of DK Bars as you wish (3 more were added to the bottom of the neck piece in Illus. J3).

Step 8: Work 6 or 7 Bead Knots (see Illus. 27) on each cord-end, to simulate beads.

Step 9: Insert the neck ring through the first and sixth picots at the top.

Conclusion

As you have learned, there are many textile crafts and innumerable objects which you can creatively combine with macramé. All you need is a working knowledge of some basic macramé knots and textile techniques, as well as an eye for unique things you can incorporate into your work.

But do not stop with the techniques and the materials specified here. Many other textile crafts have not been discussed in this book, but they offer fascinating possibilities for artistic work. For instance, try combining macramé with netting or lace-making, sprang weaving, twining or other basket techniques, stitchery, textile painting or printing. Search for unusual trinkets and decorative items to add to your work.

The results will be fascinating and a great tribute to your creative and thoughtful handicraft skills.

Suppliers

UNITED STATES

Bare Hill Studios
E. Bare Hill Road
Harvard, Massachusetts 01451

Contessa Yarns
P.O. Box 37
Lebanon, Connecticut 06249

Coulter
118 East 59th Street
New York, New York 10022

Craft Yarns of Rhode Island, Inc.
Main Street, P.O. Box 151
Harrisville, Rhode Island 02830

Durable Mfg. Co.
P.O. Box 209
Pelham, New York 10803

El Mercado Importing Co.
9002 Eighth N.E.
Seattle, Washington 98115

The Fiber Studio
P.O. Box 356
Sudbury, Massachusetts 01776

The Handweaver
460 First Street East
Sonoma, California 95476

J. L. Hammett Co.
48 Canal Street
Boston, Massachusetts 02114

Looms 'n Yarns
Box 460
Bera, Ohio 44017

The Mannings
R.D. 2
East Berlin, Pennsylvania 17316

Mexiskeins
P.O. Box 1624
Missoula, Montana 59801

The Niddy Noddy
#1 Croton Point Avenue
Croton-on-Hudson, New York 10520

Potomac Yarn Products Co.
P.O. Box 2367
Chapel Hill, North Carolina 27514

The Sheep Village
2005 Bridgeway
Sausalito, California 94965

Tahki Imports Ltd.
336 West End Avenue
New York, New York 10023

The Yarn Depot
545 Sutter Street
San Francisco, California 94102

Yarn Primitives
Box 1013
Weston, Connecticut 06880

CANADA

Briggs and Little's Woolen Mill
York Mills
Harvey Station
New Brunswick
Canada

Northwest Handcraft House
110 West Esplanade
North Vancouver, B.C.
Canada

DENMARK

CUM
Rommersgade 5
Copenhagen K, Denmark

The Danish Handicraft Guild
Vimmelskaftet 38
Copenhagen, Denmark

Julius Koch
Norrebrogade 52
Copenhagen, Denmark

ENGLAND

Arthur Beale
194 Shaftesbury Avenue
London, England

British Twines Limited
112 Green Lanes
London, England

Cuyahoga Studio
17a Hastings Road
Bexhill-on-Sea
Sussex, England

Dryad Limited
Northgates
Leicester, England

Dylon International Ltd.
139 Sydenham Road
London, S.E., England

John Lewis Limited
Oxford Street
London, England

Mace and Nairn
89 Crane Street
Salisbury
Wiltshire, England

M. Mallock & Sons
44 Vauxhall Bridge Road
London, England

The Needlewoman Shop
146–148 Regent Street
London, England

Nottingham Handcraft Company
Melton Road
West Bridgeford
Nottingham, England

FINLAND

The Friends of Finnish Handicraft
Yronkatu 13
Helsinki, Finland

Helmi Vuorelma Oy
Vesijarvenkatu 13
Lahti, Finland

Neovius Oy
Munkkisaarenkatu 2
Helsinki, Finland

NEW ZEALAND

Pauline Patton
134 Edgecumbe Road
Tauranga, New Zealand

NORWAY

Norwegian Home Arts & Crafts Association
Mollergate 4
Oslo, Norway

SWEDEN

A/B Nordiska Kompaniet
Box 7159
Stockholm, Sweden

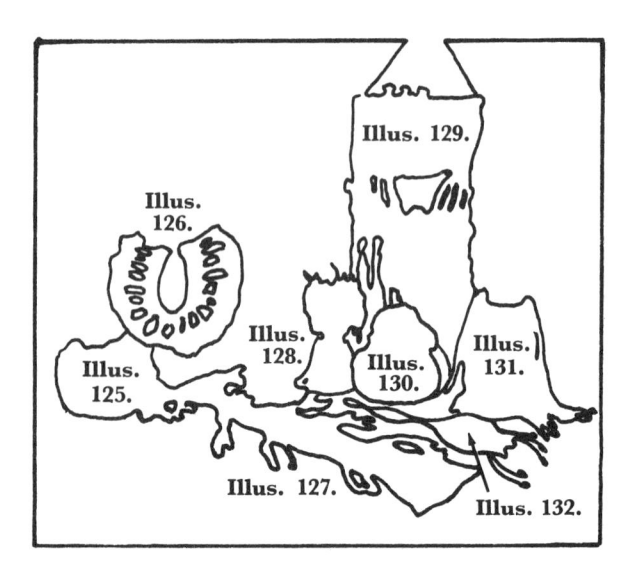

Below are descriptions of the eight projects pictured on the cover of this book. You can identify which projects are being discussed by referring to the keyed chart above.

Illus. 125. This coiled basket, made of nubby cotton-rayon yarn and decorated with macramé from spun wool yarn, is also shown in Illus. 55 and 56.

Illus. 126. This striking collar was woven on a circular cardboard loom. Wool and nubby cotton yarns were used as weft threads. The warp threads, knotted at the ends with colorful feathers, were made from marine cords.

Illus. 127. Macramé and finger weaving produced this fanciful figure made from cotton seine cords and synthetic rug yarns. This ornament is also shown in Illus. 84.

Illus. 128. Macramé, combined with wrapping and rug-hooking, using wool rug yarns and goat hair, cover the flat glass bottle used for shaping and supporting this decorative weed pot.

Illus. 129. Jute cord and rug yarns hang attractively from this magnificent hand-formed ceramic pot (by Lorraine Cilluffo). Feathers and ceramic beads (also by Lorraine Cilluffo) were worked into the macramé and the middle panel, which also contains some wrapped cords.

Illus. 130. White fur strips worked into the knotting make this macramé basket particularly striking. Synthetic rug yarn and cotton braided cord were used for the macramé. This basket is also shown in color Illus. H3.

Illus. 131. The crocheted construction which forms the foundation of this unusual sculpture was inspired by anemones. Another view of this rug yarn and mohair creation is shown in Illus. 99.

Illus. 132. Although many macramé projects are meant to be hung on walls, you can hang some around your neck. Neck pieces, like the one shown here which was made with braided rayon cords in mostly Double Knots, are fun to make because they are not very big. This neck piece is also shown in color Illus. A3.

Index

(letters indicate color pages)

adding new cords
   in weaving 47
   using Double Knot Bars 18–19
basic knots 12–23
baskets 35, H, 78
   coiled 37, 78
Bead Knot 21
   in rug-hooking 38
beads, uses of 26, 70, 71, 73–74, 78, H
bells, uses of 72
bones, uses of 71
bottles, uses of 55–56, 78
Buttonhole Knot 22–23
   Double 22–23
   Single 20, 22–23
cardboard weaving 48–49, 78
ceramics, uses of 71–72, 78, A, K
Clove Hitch 13
coiling 34–37
collar 78
Collecting Knot 21
color, use of in designing 24
conclusion 75
cords 9–11
corn husks, uses of K
crocheting 53–59, 78, A, F
decrease
   in crocheting 56
   in knitting 62
designing projects 24
Diagonal Double Knot Bars 17
Double Buttonhole Knots 22–23
Double Half Hitch 13
Double Knot (DK) 13, 16–20
Double Knot Bars 17–20
   adding new cords using 18–19
   closed 18
   Diagonal 17
   Horizontal 17
   open 18
   Vertical 18
dove-tailing in weaving 47
driftwood, uses of 71

enamelled discs, uses of 68, 70, 72, A, B, C, E, G, H, J
equipment for macramé 12–13
"fabric art" 6
feathers, uses of 26, 31, 62–66, 71, 72, 78, C, D, J, K
fibre creations 6–8
fibres 9–11
figure eight coiling 34–35
Flat Knot (FK) 13, 14–15, 20
   in rug-hooking 38
   sennits 15
flowers, uses of 71
finishing 25–26
frame-loom weaving 49
fraying cord-ends 25, 41
fringes, making 25
fur, uses of 47, 71, 73, 78, A, D, H
Ghiordes Knot 39–40
glass, uses of 72, B, F
Half Flat Knot 14, 15
Horizontal Double Knot Bars 17
horse hair, uses of 57–59
increase
   in crocheting 56
   in knitting 62
interlocking in weaving 47
jewelry, uses of 72
knitting 60–66, C, F, G
lace stitch coiling 36–37
Lark's Head Knot 22
   in rug-hooking 38–39
leaves, uses of 71
looms, types of 48–49
macramé plus
   anything 70–74
   coiling 34–37
   crocheting 53–59
   knitting 60–66
   rug-hooking 38–43
   stuffing 67–69
   weaving 44–52
   wrapping 28–35
metric conversion chart 2
moss stitch 61

neck pieces 70, 73–74, 78, A, H, J
Overhand Knot 21
plain weave 45
planning 7–8
rocks, uses of 71
rose bud, formation of 32–43
rug-hooking 25, 29, 30, 38–43, 57–59, 67, 78, B, C, D, F, G, H
sculptures 7, 57–59
seeds, uses of 6, 71
sennit 15
shells, uses of 30, 32, 35, 71, H
silver, uses of 73–74, J
Single Buttonhole Knot 20, 22–23
Square Knot (SK) 13
stockinette stitch 61
straw, uses of 31
stuffing 29, 67–69, C, E, G, H
suppliers 76–77
tabby weave 45
tapestry weave 45
tassels, making 26
tubular weaving 49
twigs, uses of 31, 71
twines 9–11
Vertical Double Knot Bars 18
wall hangings 6–7, 25, 28, 29, 41, 42–43, 44, 50–53, 62–66, 67, 68–69, A, B, C, D, E, F, G, H, J
weaving 6, 29, 44–52, B, C, D, E, G
   looms for 48–49
   plain 45
   tabby 45
   tapestry 45
weed pots 30, 32–35, 55–56, A, B, F, H
wood, uses of 72
working base 12–13
wrapping 28–35, 39, 45, 54, 55, 61, 78, A, B, C, D, F, H
yarns 9–11